Student Activities Guide

Business Principles and Management

TWELFTH EDITION

James L. Burrow, Ph.D.

Brad A. Kleindl, Ph.D.

Kenneth E. Everard, Ed.D.

THOMSON

SOUTH-WESTERN

Australia · Brazil · Canada · Mexico · Singapore · Spain · United Kingdom · United States

THOMSON

SOUTH-WESTERN

Business Principles and Management, Twelfth Edition
Student Activities Guide
James L. Burrow, Brad Kleindl, and Kenneth E. Everard

VP/Editorial Director:
Jack W. Calhoun

VP/Editor-in-Chief:
Karen Schmohe

Executive Editor:
Eve Lewis

Developmental Editor:
Karen Hein

Sr. Marketing Manager:
Nancy Long

Content Project Manager:
Diane Bowdler

Marketing Coordinator:
Angela Glassmeyer

Manager of Technology, Editorial:
Liz Prigge

Technology Project Editor:
Sally Nieman

Web Coordinator:
Ed Stubenrauch

Manufacturing Coordinator:
Kevin Kluck

Production House:
ICC Macmillan Inc.

Cover Images:
© Image Bank

Printer:
Thomson/West
Eagan, MN

CONTENTS

Chapter 1   Characteristics of Business   1

Chapter 2   Social and Ethical Environment of Business   9

Chapter 3   Economic Environment of Business   17

Chapter 4   International Environment of Business   27

Chapter 5   Proprietorships and Partnerships   35

Chapter 6   Corporate Forms of Business Ownership   45

Chapter 7   Legal Aspects of Business   53

Chapter 8   Technology and Information Management   61

Chapter 9   E-Commerce   71

Chapter 10   Organizational Communications   81

Chapter 11   Management Functions and Decision Making   91

Chapter 12   The Manager as Leader   99

Chapter 13   Planning and Organizing..   107

Chapter 14   Implementing and Controlling   115

Chapter 15   Business Financial Records   123

Chapter 16   Financing a Business   133

Chapter 17   Financial Services   143

Chapter 18   Credit and Insurance   153

Chapter 19   Product Planning and Production Management   163

Chapter 20   Nature and Scope of Marketing   171

Chapter 21   Product Development and Distribution   179

Chapter 22   Pricing and Promotion   187

Chapter 23   Managing Human Resources   197

Chapter 24   Rewarding and Developing Employees...   207

Chapter 25   Developing an Effective Organization   217

PREFACE TO THE STUDENT ACTIVITY GUIDE

This Student Activity Guide is a supplement to the Twelfth Edition of *Business Principles and Management*. It is designed to reinforce and extend your learning for each of the chapters in the textbook. A variety of types of learning activities are provided in the Student Activity Guide. Follow your teacher's instructions as you select those you will complete. You may be assigned all activities for a chapter or selected activities based on your individual learning needs. By completing the assigned tasks, you should have an excellent understanding of the principles of business and management that are presented in the textbook. Four types of exercises are provided: Study Guides, Controversial Issues, Problems, and Small Group Activities.

The Study Guide activities allow you to check your understanding of basic facts and principles by answering yes-no, multiple choice, and matching or completion questions for each chapter. Reviewing information using these types of questions will help reinforce your learning so you will remember important ideas and concepts from each chapter.

The Controversial Issues exercises challenge you to look at two questions that may be answered "yes" or "no." Business people must be open-minded and willing to consider varying ideas and viewpoints. Each Controversial Issue challenges you to consider reasons for "yes" and reasons for "no." You need to think carefully about each issue before providing reasons to support your answers. Your teacher may ask you to take one position or the other and develop a more comprehensive answer or to provide reasons for each of the possible answers—"yes" or "no." The Controversial Issues also provide an excellent opportunity for a class debate. If your teacher uses a question as a debate, he or she will provide specific instructions to you and other class members on how to prepare for and participate in the debate on the issue.

The Problems section requires you to study and solve realistic business problems related to the chapter content. Each problem is designed to use higher-order thinking skills. Many require you to complete mathematical calculations in order to answer the questions or arrive at a decision.

The Small Group Activities are the final set of activities for each chapter. These projects will likely provide you with one of the most valuable ways to learn about business. Businesses today emphasize teamwork and team decision making. The Small Group Activities present challenging business problems that should be discussed and solved by student teams. Follow your teacher's instructions in organizing study teams and completing the Small Group Activities. In some cases you will need to lead your team and in other cases serve as an effective follower and team member. In each case it is important to learn how to work well with others to develop effective solutions to business problems.

Each of the four types of activities—Study Guides, Controversial Issues, Problems, and Small Group Activities—will provide you with a different way to review and learn the textbook material. Enjoy working through the exercises assigned by your teacher as you reinforce and apply your new business knowledge.

Jim Burrow
Brad Kleindl

Study Guide

Part A—*Directions:* Indicate your answer to each of the following questions by writing either yes or no in the Answers column.

Answers

1. Are most of the businesses currently operating in the United States manufacturing firms?   1. _____
2. Do businesses vary in size from one employee to thousands of employees?   2. _____
3. Is an organization that produces or distributes a good or service for profit called a business?   3. _____
4. Do service firms produce goods?   4. _____
5. Does marketing deal with money matters related to running a business?   5. _____
6. Does the supply of a product refer to the number of similar products that will be bought at a given time and at a given price?   6. _____
7. Do industrial businesses produce goods that other businesses use to make things?   7. _____
8. Are banks and investment companies classified as industrial businesses?   8. _____
9. Because a government provides fire and police protection, can it be considered an industry?   9. _____
10. Are service businesses growing faster than production businesses?   10. _____
11. Does effectiveness occur when an organization produces needed goods or services quickly and at low cost?   11. _____
12. Are firms that are extremely efficient always very effective?   12. _____
13. Is the concept of total quality management a commitment to excellence that is accomplished by teamwork and continual improvement?   13. _____
14. Can the Malcolm Baldrige Award be presented to companies from any country?   14. _____
15. Does output refer to the quantity, or amount, produced within a given time?   15. _____
16. Has the growth in the U.S. productivity rate exceeded that of all other industrialized nations in the past few years?   16. _____
17. Do innovations refer only to the invention of new products?   17. _____
18. Has re-engineering increased customer satisfaction for most firms that use it?   18. _____
19. Is the franchisor the distributor of a franchised product or service?   19. _____
20. Does risk in business involve competition from new products?   20. _____

Total Score   _____

Answers

1. The business activity that is involved with how goods or services are exchanged between producers and consumers is (a) production, (b) marketing, (c) finance, (d) manufacturing.
   1. _____

2. Which is an example of a commercial business? (a) coal mine, (b) construction company, (c) bank, (d) car manufacturer. ....
   2. _____

3. Which industry employs the most workers in the United States? (a) agriculture, (b) government, (c) manufacturing and construction, (d) leisure and hospitality service businesses.
   3. _____

4. An important characteristic of business is that it is (a) large, (b) regulated, (c) profitable, (d) dynamic. ....
   4. _____

5. Which of the following refers to a commitment to excellence? (a) ESOP, (b) TQM, (c) GDP, (d) T&I. ....
   5. _____

6. Which of the following is NOT a result of mass production? (a) effectiveness, (b) higher cost of goods manufactured, (c) fewer workers, (d) large numbers of items produced. ....
   6. _____

7. Which of the following is NOT a way to increase efficiency? (a) increased employee wages, (b) specialization of effort, (c) better technology, (d) reorganization of work activities.......
   7. _____

8. What effect does advanced technology usually have on the cost of each item produced by a business? (a) cost stays about the same, (b) cost increases, (c) cost decreases, (d) revenue and cost break even...
   8. _____

9. How does the GDP of $12.4 trillion appear when written out? (a) $12,400, (b) $12,004,000, (c) $12,000,400,000, (d) $12,400,000,000,000. ....
   9. _____

10. In the typical franchise business, the franchisee does NOT receive (a) help in selecting a location for the business, (b) special training in how to operate efficiently, (c) guaranteed profit, (d) exclusive rights to sell in a specified geographic area. ....
    10. _____

11. Which of the following best describes risk? (a) insurance, (b) possibility of failure, (c) net losses a business suffers, (d) protection. ....
    11. _____

12. Approximately what percentage of all businesses cease operations within six to seven years of startup? (a) 10%, (b) 20%, (c) 35%, (d) 50%. ....
    12. _____

13. The two primary reasons for business failures are (a) inadequate planning and experience, (b) overexpansion and neglect, (c) economic and finance factors, (d) disaster and fraud. ....
    13. _____

14. An employee who is given funds and freedom to create a special unit or department within a company in order to develop a new product, process, or service is called an (a) apprentice, (b) entrepreneur, (c) intrapreneur, (d) investor. ....
    14. _____

15. A business that strives in all its operations to promote general welfare and observe laws is fulfilling its obligation to (a) the public, (b) its workers, (c) its investors, (d) its managers.
    15. _____

Total Score   _____

Name _____

Directions: Study each controversial issue carefully. Follow the advice of your teacher before listing in the columns provided reasons why people might answer Yes or No. Your teacher may want you to work with a class-mate, talk with others in your community to gather information, or use the library or Internet to gather facts.

1-1. In order to protect U.S. businesses from foreign competitors, should the federal government provide finan-cial assistance to businesses that are currently unable to compete globally for the purpose of reorganizing their operations to maximize efficiency?

Reasons for "Yes"	Reasons for "No"

1-2. Because the failure rate among new businesses is high, should potential entrepreneurs be required to demonstrate that they have the knowledge of how to run a successful business before being allowed to own one?

Reasons for "Yes"	Reasons for "No"

PROBLEMS

1-A. Check the column that correctly classifies whether each business listed below is an industrial business or a commercial business.

		Commercial	Industrial
1.	Crushed stone mill	____	____
2.	Credit card business	____	____
3.	Sporting goods shop	____	____
4.	Home building firm	____	____
5.	Health care center	____	____

1-B. For each of the activities listed below, check the column that indicates whether the activity applies primarily to effectiveness or efficiency. Assume your company operates a lawn-mowing service and must compete with four other companies.

		Effectiveness	Efficiency
1.	Ask customers what they like most and least about your service.	____	____
2.	Buy new equipment to prevent lost mowing time from breakdowns.	____	____
3.	Mow all lawns located near each other on the same day.	____	____
4.	Add new services such as fertilizing and watering lawns.	____	____
5.	Lower your operating costs by buying gas in quantity at lower prices.	____	____
6.	Sharpen blades more often to improve appearance of grass.	____	____
7.	Train your workers in customer courtesy.	____	____

1-C. The wealth of a nation can be shown in rates per thousand persons owning selected appliances. Using the information shown below collected from several countries in a recent year, answer the questions provided.

Appliance	U.S.	Denmark	Germany	Japan	China
Radio	2115	1146	946	957	195
Computer	407	360	256	202	6
Television	805	592	564	684	319
Mobile Phone	206	273	99	304	10

1. Based on the appliances owned, in which country is the standard of living the highest? _____

   the lowest? _____

2. Based on the appliances owned, which country has the second-best standard of living? _____

3. Which appliance is the most popular in most countries? _____

4. Given the "rates per thousand people," how would you explain why the number of radios shown for the

   U.S. and Denmark exceeds one thousand?

   _____

   _____

   _____

1-D. Place a check in the column that shows the form of business ownership that best identifies the situation described.

	Franchise	Intrapraneurship	Entrepreneurship
1. An experienced employee purchases the right to operate a business in a specific location from the owner of the business concept, who agrees to provide help in planning and operating the new business.	____	____	____
2. An employee sells all of her shares of a company's stock in order to start a business of her own.	____	____	____
3. Three workers agree to work separately from the other business employees to create a new process for increasing output and improving quality.	____	____	____
4. Two workers leave a company to form their own business that will produce a new product they have agreed to sell to their former business.	____	____	____

1-E. Are you the kind of person who could start a business and make it go? Here is a way to find out. For each question below, check the answer that says what you feel or comes closest to it. Be honest with yourself.

1. *Are you a self-starter?*
____ I do things on my own. Nobody must tell me to get going.
____ If someone gets me started, I keep going all right.
____ Easy does it. I do not put myself out until I have to.

2. *How do you feel about other people?*
____ I like people. I can get along with just about anybody.
____ I have plenty of friends—I do not need anyone else.
____ Most people irritate me.

3. *Can you lead others?*
____ I can get most people to follow when I start something.
____ I can give the orders if someone tells me what we should do.
____ I let someone else get things moving. Then I go along if I feel like it.

4. *Can you take responsibility?*
____ I like to take charge of things and see them through.
____ I will take over if I have to, but I would rather let someone else be responsible.
____ There are always some "eager beavers" around wanting to show how smart they are. I say let them be responsible.

5. *How good an organizer are you?*
____ I like to have a plan before I start. I am usually the one to get things lined up when the group wants to do something.
____ I do all right unless things get too confusing. Then I quit.
____ I get all set and then something comes along and presents too many problems. So I just take things as they come.

6. *How good a worker are you?*
____ I can keep going as long as I need to. I do not mind working hard for something I want.
____ I will work hard for a while, but when I have had enough, that's it.
____ I do not believe that hard work gets you anywhere.

7. *Can you make decisions?*
___ I can make up my mind in a hurry if I have to. It usually turns out okay, too.
___ I can make decisions if I have plenty of time. If I have to make up my mind quickly, I later think I should have decided the other way.
___ I do not like to be the one who has to decide things.

8. *Can people trust what you say?*
___ You bet they can. I do not say things I do not mean.
___ I try to be honest most of the time, but sometimes I just say what is easiest.
___ Why bother if the other person does not know the difference?

9. *Can you stick with it?*
___ If I make up my mind to do something, I do not let anything stop me.
___ I usually finish what I start—if it goes well.
___ If it does not go right at the start, I quit. Why beat your brains out?

10. *How good is your health?*
___ I never run down!
___ I have enough energy for most things I want to do.
___ I run out of energy sooner than most of my friends seem to.

Count the checks you made. They should add to 10.

How many checks are there beside the first answer to each question? _____

How many checks are there beside the second answer to each question? _____

How many checks are there beside the third answer to each question? _____

If most of your checks are beside the first answers, you probably have what it takes to run a business. If not, you are likely to have more trouble than you can handle by yourself. Better find a partner who is strong where you are weak. If many checks are beside the third answer, you should not consider going into business for yourself without making some major changes. You will be better off working for someone else as an employee.

1-F. Many newly opened active businesses are started each year. Study the information given for a year. Then answer the questions below.

No. of Employees	No. of Firms	Percent of Firms
2 or fewer	135,010	_____
3 to 5	53,230	_____
6 to 10	24,902	_____
11 to 20	11,204	_____
21 or more	9,364	_____
Total	_____	_____

1. How many businesses were started during the year? Record your answer in the space provided.
2. For the number of employees in each category shown, what is the percent of new startups involved? Record your answer in the space provided.
3. What percent of the total businesses that started have fewer than six employees? _____
4. Based on the figures above and your answers to the questions asked, place a check on the line provided ONLY if the statement is correct.

   a. The majority of newly started businesses have two or fewer employees. _____

   b. Less than one percent of the newly started businesses have six or more employees. _____

   c. Over eighty percent of the newly started businesses have five or fewer employees. _____

1-G. Ten years ago, Raul and Sangita Patel started a small restaurant that sold mostly seafood. The high quality of the food, fair prices, and an attractive dining room caused the business to become very successful. Two years after the first restaurant was opened, they opened an identical restaurant for their oldest daughter to operate in a nearby community. This restaurant was also successful. Today the Patels have five restaurants, and each is doing well.

The Patels would like to continue opening restaurants in other nearby communities. However, they know they cannot operate any more restaurants because even now their time is much too limited. For that reason, they have been thinking of other ways to expand their business. A friend, Jason Johnson, suggested that they start a franchise and he be given the first chance to operate one of the restaurants in a nearby state.

1. Do you think operating under a franchise arrangement will work for the Patels? Yes _____ No _____

    Why? _____

    _____

2. If the Patels gave Jason Johnson the opportunity to open a restaurant under a franchise agreement, who

    would be the franchisor? _____

3. Who would be the franchisee? _____

4. List some of the kinds of help that the Patels might provide Jason Johnson under a franchise agreement.

    _____

    _____

    _____

5. How will the Patels benefit by franchising their restaurants to people such as Jason Johnson?

    _____

    _____

6. How can the Patels control the way others run their franchised restaurants?

    _____

    _____

    _____

SMALL GROUP ACTIVITIES

Businesses have spent a great deal of time and money attempting to become more effective and more efficient. They have tried new approaches as described in the chapter, including the empowering of workers. Could schools empower students to become more effective and efficient? In this exercise you are being empowered to assist your school in making the learning process more effective and efficient.

With instructions from your teacher, form groups of four students. Each group of four should further divide into pairs. One pair of students in each group will focus on identifying effective and efficient ways to improve learning about business *in school*. The other pair in each group will focus on effective and efficient ways to improve learning about business *at home*. Follow the steps below.

Group Activity 1

1. With your partner, create two lists on separate sheets of paper. Label the first list *Effectiveness* and the second *Efficiency*.

2. Decide which pair of students in your group will focus on learning in school and which will focus on learning at home.

3. With your partner, offer specific suggestions for how learning could be improved. Do not discuss the ideas at this point—just record them on the list that best characterizes the idea: *Effectiveness* or *Efficiency*. Your goal is to generate as many ideas as possible within the time allotted by your instructor. Some examples for school-learning and home-learning ideas appear below.

4. When you complete your list, record the number of items you generated.

School-Learning Examples:
1. "I think one businessperson should be invited to answer student questions after students have learned the material in each chapter." Action: Don't discuss this now, but record it on the *Effectiveness* list.

2. "I don't think the teacher should waste class time dealing with unimportant things—things we may already know or have no interest in knowing." Action: Don't discuss, but record it on the *Efficiency* list.

Home-Learning Examples:
1. "I think all study should be done at home in a quiet place without interruptions from anyone." Action: Don't discuss, but record it on the *Effective* list.

2. "I want to limit my homework to one hour per day or less." Action: Don't discuss, but record it on the *Efficiency* list.

Group Activity 2

1. Each pair of students should now meet with the other pair in their group of four. Together, discuss your group's *Effectiveness* lists and combine them into one list for the group. First, decide whether each item is correctly classified as *effective* or *efficient*. You may have to move some items from one list to the other. If necessary, improve the wording to clarify the idea.

2. Now rank the items in your group's combined list into these categories: most important, somewhat important, and least important. Provide reasons for your answers.

3. Repeat Steps 1 and 2 above for the *Efficiency* list.

4. After completing Steps 1 through 3, report to the class the "most important" items on your *Effectiveness* and *Efficiency* lists with reasons for your answers.

Chapter 2		Scoring Record				
Social and Ethical Environment of Business	Name _____ Date _____		Part A	Part B	Part C	Total
		Perfect score	20	10	5	35
		My score				

Study Guide

Part A—*Directions:* Indicate your answer to each of the following questions by writing either yes or no in the Answers column.

Answers

1. Does the United States have the world's largest economy?... 1. _____

2. Do changes in population as well as changes in lifestyles directly affect business operations? .... 2. _____

3. In order for living standards to improve, must the country's population grow at a faster rate than its GDP?... 3. _____

4. Must a business consider both the size of the population and the characteristics of the population during its planning process?.. 4. _____

5. Is a country's population growth rate controlled mostly by its birth, death, and immigration rates?... 5. _____

6. Did the "baby bust" period create an increased supply of workers?.............................. 6. _____

7. Will a business that specializes in selling goods for a particular age group be affected if the number of people in that age group greatly increases or decreases?....................... 7. _____

8. Is the labor force defined as most people aged 16 or over who are available for work, whether employed or unemployed? .... 8. _____

9. In the last three decades, did the labor participation rate for women decrease? .... 9. _____

10. Has one of the problems of America's economy been its inability to create new jobs? .... 10. _____

11. Has the demand for skilled workers been falling? .... 11. _____

12. Were recent high school graduates particularly deficient in math, computer, social, and communication skills? .... 12. _____

13. Has the United States Bureau of the Census found that about 25 percent of the population live in poverty?.. 13. _____

14. Is the invisible barrier to job advancement referred to as the glass ceiling?................... 14. _____

15. If male carpenters and female construction workers require the same level of training and responsibility, should the pay scale be higher for males with families?............................ 15. _____

16. Does productivity tend to drop when employees regularly switch jobs within the organization? .... 16. _____

17. Are resources such as natural gas, oil, and iron ore in unlimited supply? .... 17. _____

18. When a business changes from natural gas to coal, does it meet environmental goals but violate conservation goals? .... 18. _____

19. Does "ethics" refer to standards of moral conduct that individuals and groups set for themselves? .... 19. _____

20. Does the American Civil Liberties Union examine workplace discrimination practices? ... 20. _____

Total Score _____

Part B—*Directions:* For each of the following statements, select the word, or group of words, that best completes the statement. In the Answers column, write the letter corresponding to the answer selected.

1. The north central and northeastern states where manufacturing firms once dominated is known as the (a) frost belt, (b) sun belt, (c) rust belt, (d) snow belt. .... 1. _____

2. In a recent year, the Bureau of Labor Statistics reported that the size of the American labor force was almost (a) 140 million, (b) 115 million, (c) 90 million, (d) 65 million. .... 2. _____

3. In 2005, the labor participation rate for women reached about (a) 50%, (b) 60%, (c) 70%, (d) 80%. .... 3. _____

4. Over the years, the labor participation rate for men has (a) increased greatly, (b) increased slowly, (c) stayed about the same, (d) dropped slightly. .... 4. _____

5. With improved technology in recent years, the demand for skilled workers has (a) increased, (b) decreased a little, (c) remained about the same, (d) decreased a great deal. ..... 5. _____

6. Which statement about the workforce is INCORRECT? (a) Women and racial minorities sometimes find it hard to be promoted above a certain level. (b) Many states have passed laws that promote using comparable worth for determining wages in government jobs. (c) Wages tend to be lower in jobs that employ lots of men than in jobs held primarily by women. (d) The rapid growth in the computer industry has led to high wages for those with the necessary education and skills. .... 6. _____

7. Which of the following is NOT a factor in determining comparable worth? (a) Requiring special skills for a job. (b) Requiring certain educational backgrounds for a job. (c) Requiring certain physical ability for a job. (d) Requiring males or females for a job. .... 7. _____

8. Which of the following is an INCORRECT statement regarding what employers are doing to attract and retain competent workers? (a) Improve the way work is done. (b) Assure healthier and safer working conditions. (c) Help workers deal with personal problems. (d) Train workers to like repetitive jobs. .... 8. _____

9. Which statement about the human factor in business is FALSE? (a) Employees want more variety in their work. (b) Employees want more opportunity to participate in decisions that affect their working lives. (c) Employees do not want to work in teams. (d) Employees want more on-the-job responsibility. .... 9. _____

10. Which statement is INCORRECT about ethical issues? (a) One good approach for handling ethical issues is to select the behavior that does the most good for the most people. (b) Notions of what is right and wrong do not change over time. (c) Ethical issues arise when firms must choose ethical practices of a foreign country or of their own country. (d) Ethical issues arise when it is not clear whether a particular action is legal or illegal. ... 10. _____

Total Score _____

Part C—*Directions:* Below are listed several kinds of pollution. Indicate how each type of pollution should be classified by placing a check mark in the appropriate column.

	Water Pollution	Air Pollution	Land Pollution
1. Exhaust being discharged by automobile engines.			
2. Chemicals being dumped from a house into a sewer line.			
3. Oil being spilled while being transported by an ocean liner.			
4. A town's trash being dumped into an abandoned stone quarry.			
5. Fish being killed by waste from a factory.			

Directions: Study each controversial issue carefully. Follow the advice of your teacher before listing in the columns provided reasons why people might answer Yes or No. Your teacher may want you to work with a classmate, talk with others in your community to gather information, or use the library or Internet to gather facts.

2-1. Because most jobs require more skills than in the past, should the minimum amount of education be raised to 18 years or a high school diploma?

Reasons for "Yes"	Reasons for "No"

2-2. Should all firms be required to use the CERES Principles rather than practicing the principles only on a voluntary basis? (The CERES Principles appear in the textbook on page 45.)

Reasons for "Yes"	Reasons for "No"

PROBLEMS

2-A. Assume that there are 92 million people who work in or near cities in the United States. Study the categories of jobs held by these people and answer the questions that follow. The figures are shown in millions of workers.

Clerical	15.8		Machinists	5.5
Professional	13.6		Technicians	3.6
Managerial	12.2		Transportation	3.4
Sales	11.2		Laborers	3.4
Precision crafts	9.9		Others	3.4
Service	9.9			

1. What percent of the workforce applies to each of the top four job categories?
   a. Clerical .... _____

   b. Professional .... _____

   c. Managerial .... _____

   d. Sales .... _____

2. About what percent of the workforce do the top four job categories combined represent? .... _____

3. Which one job do you believe would be *most* likely to be held mainly by females? .... _____

4. Which one job do you believe would be *least* likely to be held mainly by females? .... _____

5. Which one job is *most* likely to be held by people with the fewest job skills? .... _____

2-B. Assume the "baby busters" (busters) who were aged 30–41 in a recent year were compared with the entire population. The estimated breakdown by race is shown. Study the statistics and answer the questions that appear below the table. (Note: Hispanics are also classified as Caucasian; therefore, totals will exceed 100%.)

	Baby Busters	Total Population
Caucasian	81.2%	83.5%
African American	14.0	12.4
American Indian	.9	.8
Asian	3.9	3.3
Hispanic	12.3	9.5

1. What is the percentage difference of Caucasian busters in relation to the total Caucasian population? .... _____

2. What is the percentage difference of African American busters in relation to the total African American population? .... _____

3. Which race has the greatest percentage difference? .... _____

   What is the percentage difference? .... _____

4. What conclusion can be made about the difference between Caucasian busters and other busters?

   _____

   _____

   _____

2-C. Assume that the percent of the entire U.S. population living below the poverty level was 14.2 percent. Shown below are poverty levels for a sample of states. Study the figures and answer the questions.

Michigan	14.1%
Mississippi	23.3%
Montana	15.4%
Nevada	11.4%
New Hampshire	7.3%
New Mexico	22.4%
Wisconsin	9.9%

1. Which states are in the Frost Belt?

_____

2. Which states are in the Sun Belt?

_____

3. Which state can be most considered a Rust Belt state? _____

4. What is the average poverty level for the states shown? _____

5. How many times greater is the poverty level in Mississippi compared to New Hampshire's poverty level?

_____

6. For the states shown, is the poverty level higher in the Frost Belt or the Sun Belt?

_____

_____

_____

2-D. Assume the yearly differences in pay between men and women with college degrees by age groups differ as shown below. Study the figures and answer the questions.

Age Group	Men	Women	Percent of Women's Pay to Men's Pay
18–24	$22,300	$20,500	_____
25–34	33,900	25,500	_____
35–44	44,700	28,900	_____
45–54	50,200	29,600	_____
55–64	54,600	29,600	_____

1. Calculate the percent of women's pay to men's pay and record your answers in the answer lines above.

2. Provide three major reasons why the percent of women's pay to men's drops throughout one's working life.

_____

_____

_____

_____

_____

2-E. How aware are you of your environment? Answer the following questions as truthfully as possible about yourself and your family. Write either yes or no for each question in the Answers column. When you finish, check your environmental awareness score following the test.

Answers

1. Does your home or apartment have storm windows? .... _____
2. Do your doors and windows have weather stripping or caulking? .... _____
3. Is the thermostat lowered to 65 degrees or less when you go to bed? .... _____
4. Do you turn off unnecessary lights when they are not being used? .... _____
5. Is the thermostat in your home set no higher than 68 or 70 degrees when someone is there during the day? .... _____
6. Do you turn the water off while you brush your teeth? .... _____
7. Do you drink a glass of water immediately without running the water awhile first? .... _____
8. Are you aware that less water is used in a quick shower than in a bath? .... _____
9. Are you aware that a self-defrosting refrigerator costs 25 percent more to operate? .... _____
10. Is there usually someone watching your television set while it is on? .... _____
11. Do you place plastic containers, tins, newspapers, and magazines in recycling containers instead of throwing them in the garbage? .... _____
12. Do you use a regular blanket rather than an electric blanket? .... _____
13. Is your family car (or cars) regularly maintained? .... _____
14. Do you use sand rather than salt on icy roads, driveways, or sidewalks? .... _____
15. When you take out fast food, do you regularly put the waste packaging such as wrappers and paper cups in waste containers? .... _____
16. Do you compost leaves, grass clippings, and kitchen vegetable waste? .... _____
17. When you buy your first car (or next car), will it be an economy car? .... _____
18. Are you upset when you see litter, such as bottles, cans, and paper, strewn about in your community? .... _____
19. Do you discourage excessive purchase of food, clothes, and other items that you do not need? _____
20. Do you, or would you, car pool to work? .... _____

Count the number of *yes* answers and place your total score here. .... _____

        If your total score is 16–20, you are *very alert* to your environment.

        If your total score is 12–15, you are *fairly alert* to your environment.

        If your total score is 8–11, you are *somewhat alert* to your environment.

        If your total score is 0–7, you are *not alert* to your environment.

2-F. Businesses must be ethically responsible. For each situation, decide whether each business is "ethical" or "unethical." Write your answer in the Answers column and give a reason for your decision.

Answers

1. Because the cost of hiring a firm to dispose of waste liquids from a paint manufacturing firm is so high, a company daily dumps a small amount into a nearby large river. The president knows that a very large business nearby also does this. "If they can do it, so can we," he says. .... _____

_____

_____

_____

2. A large company that sells apple juice and advertises it as "fresh" finds itself in financial difficulty. It decides to keep running the same ad but use imitation rather than real apple juice because people cannot tell the difference in taste. This action would allow the business to make enough profit to survive without having to let go of some workers and cut other costs. .... _____

_____

_____

_____

3. Each December a small entrepreneur gives a sizable cash Christmas gift to key city officials with the hope that when special favors are needed, these officials will readily grant them. This is a fairly common practice in this community. .... _____

_____

_____

_____

_____

2-G. Read the following story and answer the questions that follow.

For years the Gumshoe Company has been doing rather well making house slippers for distribution by a large department store chain. Its 200 workers come from the small city of 75,000 in which the plant is located. Over 150 of the workers are women, most of whom work in the plant's cutting, sewing, and packaging departments. About 25 men work in the receiving and shipping department. There are about ten supervisors and managers, all of whom are males. The rest of the employees are office, maintenance, and design people. Last week the plant manager, Barry Danziger, received the following memo:

> Sir: For too long this company has been run by men who keep women in their place. Sexist comments are heard frequently and, worst of all, not a single woman holds a management position. None of us is ever considered for a supervisory position when an opening occurs. Someone from the shipping and receiving department always gets it. We expect the next supervisory position that opens to be filled by a woman, or you will immediately see that we mean business.
>
> Women's Rights Committee

Mr. Danziger asked the present supervisors what they knew about the matter. None had heard anything. Some of the more outspoken women workers were also contacted. All remained silent. Barry Danziger was puzzled. All management openings are announced through a newsletter and posted on plant bulletin boards. When the last opening occurred, not a single woman applied.

1. What action could the women take to show management that they "mean business"?

_____

_____

_____

2. Give two possible reasons why no woman applied for the last supervisory position.

_____

_____

_____

3. If no women from the plant apply for the next position, what should the plant manager do?

_____

_____

_____

2-H. Assume you are an employee in a company where the business situations described below have occurred. Decide whether each situation is "ethical" or "unethical." Write your answer in the Answers column and give a reason for your decision.

1. A coworker was absent from work yesterday to visit a friend but plans to report it as an illness. .... _____

2. Your boss plans to overstate your department's output so that she will win the Manager of the Month award. .... _____

3. You learn that the business has an old warehouse that is no longer needed for storage. Management has decided to make offices there for fifty clerks. The building's walls have asbestos that could harm workers over time. .... _____

4. A product your firm makes is dangerous to users, but the firm plans to take no action to make the item safe. .... _____

5. Another employee has been using illegal drugs on the job and the supervisor does not know about it. .... _____

6. A salesperson has the use of a company car, but you have seen the car used on weekends for personal use. .... _____

7. A highly qualified African American worker applied for an opening as a supervisor but was rejected in favor of a less-qualified Caucasian candidate. .... _____

8. A less-qualified African American male was promoted to a managerial position over a more highly qualified Caucasian female. .... _____

Study Guide

Part A—*Directions:* Indicate your answer to each of the following questions by writing either yes or no in the Answers column.

Answers

1. Is "economics" the body of knowledge that relates to producing and using goods and services to satisfy human wants? .... 1. _____

2. Does the school cafeteria provide for an economic want? .... 2. _____

3. Does our economic system satisfy all the wants of the people? .... 3. _____

4. Does a retail grocer provide both time utility and place utility? .... 4. _____

5. Is a robot on a car assembly line an example of a consumer good? .... 5. _____

6. Are capital goods needed to produce consumer goods and services? .... 6. _____

7. Can a country produce as many capital goods as it wishes to produce at any one time? ..... 7. _____

8. If the production of consumer goods increases, must the production of capital goods and services also increase? .... 8. _____

9. Are countries that adopt a market economy often dictatorships? .... 9. _____

10. Does privatization occur when a government provides a good or service that was formerly provided by a business? .... 10. _____

11. As the demand for a product decreases, does the price of the product usually increase? ..... 11. _____

12. Can a change in the demand or the supply of a product cause a change in the price of a product? .... 12. _____

13. Do consumers help decide what will be produced as well as how much will be produced? 13. _____

14. Is competition among businesses limited mainly to price competition? .... 14. _____

15. Is it necessary to expand only the production of goods and services for economic growth to occur? .... 15. _____

16. Does production decrease and unemployment increase during recessions? .... 16. _____

17. Is a recession a decline in the GDP that continues for six months or more? ...... 17. _____

18. Does inflation result in a decline in the purchasing power of money? .... 18. _____

19. During inflation, does the dollar buy more than it did before inflation? .... 19. _____

20. Does the lowering and raising of taxes by the federal government aid in controlling recession and inflation? .... 20. _____

Total Score _____

Part B—*Directions:* For each of the following statements, select the word, or group of words, that best completes the statement. In the Answers column, write the letter corresponding to the answer selected.

1. Which of the following is NOT considered an economic want? (a) want for a television set, (b) want for medical attention, (c) want for friendship, (d) want for new clothing. ..... 1. _____

2. A shoe manufacturer creates (a) form utility, (b) time utility, (c) place utility, (d) economic utility. .... 2. _____

3. The basic factors of production are (a) land (natural resources) and labor; (b) land (natural resources), labor, and capital goods; (c) land (natural resources), labor, capital goods, and entrepreneurship; (d) capital goods and labor. .... 3. _____

4. When the production of consumer goods decreases, the production of (a) capital goods increases, (b) capital goods decreases and services increases, (c) capital goods decreases, (d) capital goods and services decreases. .... 4. _____

5. Machines used to make automobiles are classified as (a) consumer goods, (b) capital goods, (c) consumer services, (d) domestic goods. .... 5. _____

6. In which type of economy do individual buying decisions in the marketplace together determine what, how, and for whom goods and services will be produced? (a) communistic, (b) command, (c) market, (d) mixed. .... 6. _____

7. What type of economy is China attempting to move toward? (a) capital, (b) command, (c) market, (d) mixed. .... 7. _____

8. The term that best describes our present economic/political system is (a) socialism, (b) communism, (c) capitalism, (d) privatization. .... 8. _____

9. Approximately what percent of total receipts represents the average net profit of all business firms? (a) 5%, (b) 10%, (c) 15%, (d) 25%. .... 9. _____

10. Demand for a product is the (a) same as want, (b) price at which the product will sell most readily, (c) number of products that will be bought at a given time at a given price, (d) number of future customers. .... 10. _____

11. Prices are determined by the forces of (a) supply only, (b) demand only, (c) both supply and demand, (d) business cycles. .... 11. _____

12. Nonprice competition occurs when a firm (a) takes business away from its competitors by lowering prices, (b) conducts an extensive advertising campaign to convince the public that its product is better than all other brands, (c) does not have to compete with other sellers for consumer dollars, (d) occurs only when service is provided. .... 12. _____

13. Economic growth occurs when a country produces goods and services at (a) the same rate the population is increasing, (b) a faster rate than the population is increasing, (c) a slower rate than the population is increasing, (d) the same rate unemployment is increasing. ..... 13. _____

14. The Consumer Price Index (CPI) is (a) the total market value of all goods produced and services purchased in a year, (b) the total of all the products that are purchased at a given time, (c) a measure of the average change in prices of consumer goods and services, (d) the same as the Economic Index of Leading Indicators. .... 14. _____

15. Which of the following is NOT likely to occur during a recession? (a) decreased production, (b) increased unemployment, (c) increased demand for goods and services, (d) decline in GDP. .... 15. _____

Total Score _____

18

Directions: Study each controversial issue carefully. Follow the advice of your teacher before listing in the columns provided reasons why people might answer Yes or No. Your teacher may want you to work with a classmate, talk with others in your community to gather information, or use the library or Internet to gather facts.

3-1. Should the federal government privatize the U.S. Postal Service?

Reasons for "Yes"	Reasons for "No"

3-2. To encourage savings and, in turn, capital formation, should the interest earned by individuals on savings and other investments NOT be taxed by the federal government?

Reasons for "Yes"	Reasons for "No"

PROBLEMS

3-A. In economics, *utility* is the ability of a good or service to satisfy a want. For each of the four common types of utility shown in the columns below, check the one type of utility that best fits the situation described.

Situation	Form	Place	Time	Possession
1. You go to a nearby store to buy a canvas walking shoe, but the store carries leather only.	_____	_____	_____	_____
2. You have just completed signing the rental form for the use of a portable computer to take on a business trip.	_____	_____	_____	_____
3. You dash into a bookstore on your lunch hour and ask for this week's best-selling novel by name, which the clerk has in stock.	_____	_____	_____	_____
4. You were planning to walk home after a movie, but it is raining so you look for a taxi. One pulls up as you leave the theater.	_____	_____	_____	_____

Types of Utility (column group header)

3-B. For each item listed below, determine whether it is a capital good or a consumer good. Check the appropriate column.

	Capital Good	Consumer Good
1. Bulldozer for building contractors	_____	_____
2. Garden hose	_____	_____
3. Home	_____	_____
4. Factory	_____	_____
5. Machine for making bicycles	_____	_____

3-C. On the line provided, write the name of the economic system that best represents each statement.

1. Resources are allocated by government only. _____

2. Marketing decisions are made by market conditions. _____

3. China is a good example of this economic system. _____

4. Businesses and individuals own natural resources and capital goods. _____

5. Government controls business decisions extensively for the allocation of some resources, but has little

   control over distribution. _____

3-D. For each economic-political system listed, check the column that best fits its characteristics.

	Capitalism	Socialism	Communism
1. Freedom to own land and other property.	____	____	____
2. Usually a shortage of consumer goods.	____	____	____
3. Some industries owned by government but often allows some private ownership.	____	____	____
4. Nearly any individual may start a business.	____	____	____
5. Government decides how and what goods are to be produced.	____	____	____

3-E. Below are a few average prices shown in Year 3 dollars for goods and services for three different time periods. Study the figures and answer the questions.

	In Year 3 Dollars		
	Year 1	Year 2	Year 3
Gallon of gas	1.55	1.26	1.12
Movie ticket (New York City)	2.75	5.74	5.05
Television (color)	1,432*	1,466	220
Hospital cost for one day	108	332	752
Eggs (one dozen)	3.77	2.54	.89
Postage (first-class letter)	.16	.26	.29

*Only available in black and white.

1. Which items declined in price from Year 1 to Year 3? _____

2. What economic factors might have most influenced the price of the items that declined in price?

   _____

3. Provide a possible reason why the price of movie tickets went up in Year 2 but dropped in Year 3.

   _____

4. If car manufacturers produce engines that use half as much gas, what might happen to the price of gas a

   few years from now? _____

5. By what percent did the cost of eggs decrease from Year 1 to Year 3?

   _____

6. By what percent did the cost of postage on a first-class letter increase from Year 1 to Year 3?

   _____

3-F. Study the Consumer Price Index figures below for two different years. Then answer the questions below.

	Year 5[*]	Year 15[*]
Food and beverages	188.0	302.0
Housing	164.5	349.9
Apparel and upkeep	142.3	206.0
Transportation	150.6	319.9
Medical care	168.6	403.1
Entertainment	152.2	265.0
Other goods and services	153.9	326.6

In Year 1, the CPI was 100.

1. Which item had the greatest increase in the CPI during the ten-year period?

   _____

2. Which item had the least increase in the CPI during the decade?

   _____

3. As the CPI increases, does the purchasing power of the dollar increase, decrease, or stay about the same?

   _____

4. What types of people are hurt most by rapid increases in the CPI?

   _____

5. Are increases in the CPI a measure of the rate of inflation, recession, or depression? _____

3-G. If the national economy grows too fast, the result may be inflation. But if it grows too slowly, a recession or a depression is likely to occur. The federal government may take different actions that can help control the economy by controlling the rate of growth. Place a check in one of the columns on the right to show the expected effect of each governmental action on the economy.

Governmental Action	Speeds Economic Growth	Slows Economic Growth	No Effect on Economic Growth
1. Raising federal income taxes	_____	_____	_____
2. Lowering federal income taxes	_____	_____	_____
3. Increasing government spending for transportation	_____	_____	_____
4. Reducing government spending for defense	_____	_____	_____
5. Launching a new satellite to the planet Venus	_____	_____	_____
6. Passing a new law to lower the voting age	_____	_____	_____

Name _____

3-H. Most nations experience business cycles. Check the appropriate business cycle phase shown in the columns on the right with the situation described on the left.

Economic Situation	Expansion	Peak	Contraction	Trough
1. A period when unemployment is at its worst	___	___	___	___
2. A period of high employment and rising wages and prices	___	___	___	___
3. A period called depression	___	___	___	___
4. A period just before the unemployment rate starts to climb	___	___	___	___
5. A period of runaway inflation	___	___	___	___
6. A period when prices stop rising and graduates begin to find it more difficult to land jobs	___	___	___	___

3-I. Obtain three brands of ballpoint pens, or some other low-priced product that most people buy from time to time. Select brands that differ in price, color, size, or shape. Ask ten people which item they would buy if they needed a pen and if these were the only choices. Once each person has selected the brand, ask for the main reason for the selection. Record the information in forms set up similar to the table below. Then compile your results here.

	Brand A	Brand B	Brand C
Brand or product preference:	___	___	___

Main reason for selecting Brand A, Brand B, or Brand C

	Brand A	Brand B	Brand C
Price	___	___	___
Color	___	___	___
Size	___	___	___
Shape	___	___	___
Quality	___	___	___
Reputation of company	___	___	___
Other (write in) _____	___	___	___

1. Which brand was the most popular? _____

2. Which brand was the least popular? _____

3. What was the main reason for selecting the most popular brand? _____

_____

4. Did price or nonprice competition most often influence potential buyers? _____

SMALL GROUP ACTIVITIES

Group Activity 1

In this activity you will compare current prices of common household products with prices ten years ago. Your instructor will place you into small groups of two to three students. The task of your group is to select three common household products used by a typical family. Each group member is to pick a different store to obtain product prices. The group should then average the prices from the different stores.

Using the Internet or the library, find what those same or similar products cost ten years ago. Now compare the average current and former prices and calculate the percent of increase or decrease. Each group is to report the "inflationary rates" for its products for the ten-year period to the class.

Group Activity 2

Your teacher will place you in one of three groups. Each group will represent one of the three fictitious nations that are described below. Each nation will experience economic conditions during different time periods. As members of your nation's top economic council, your group must make recommendations to your government leaders and provide them with reasons for your suggestions. Here are the groups:

Group A: This group represents the country of Algoon. It is a struggling third-world communistic agricultural nation. Algoon has only a few manufacturing firms. Its population is relatively poor, and a dictator rules this command economy. Your group aids the ruler in declaring economic policy.

Group B: The group represents the country of Bazoon. It is a somewhat backward but fast-growing country economically. Bazoon has plenty of natural resources, and many developed countries want those resources. Its government is socialistic, and its economic system is mixed. Your group helps the government make economic decisions.

Group C: This group represents the nation of Capsoon. It is large in size with a variety of industrial and service firms. Its population is economically well off. While it has many citizens who are considered poor, even the poor are generally better off than the average citizens of Algoon and Bazoon. It is a democratic nation that has primarily a market economy. Your group advises the government in economic matters.

Problems and Decisions:

Each country's economic council will offer advice, with reasons, to its nation's leaders for how to accomplish the following tasks in keeping strictly with its economic and political system.

1. A recession has existed during the last six months. Offer the leader advice on what to do to turn your economy around. Why does your council feel this is good advice?

2. The unemployment rate is so high that some people are dying of starvation or freezing to death because they cannot afford heat, food, and winter clothing. Recommend immediate corrective economic measures that will get your country out of a major depression.

3. Runaway inflation is creating problems for everyone, especially retirees. The value of their retirement savings has diminished greatly. What can your council do to stabilize your economy?

Chapter 4		Scoring Record				
International Environment of Business	Name _____ Date _____		Part A	Part B	Part C	Total
		Perfect score	20	10	5	35
		My score				

Study Guide

Part A—*Directions:* Indicate your answer to each of the following questions by writing either yes or no in the Answers column.

1. Have trade patterns on an international level shifted from services to goods? .... 1. _____
2. Is buying goods and services made in other countries called *importing*? .... 2. _____
3. Do Americans export goods from France when they buy French perfume? .... 3. _____
4. Is a *parent firm* a business that owns or controls production or service facilities in more than one country? .... 4. _____
5. Are most of the world's smallest corporations multinationals? .... 5. _____
6. Is one reason for imposing tariffs to earn revenue for the country? .... 6. _____
7. Does dumping lower the price of goods sold in a foreign market? .... 7. _____
8. Do quotas limit the number of goods permitted to enter a country? .... 8. _____
9. Do tariffs raise the price of foreign products? .... 9. _____
10. Do nontariff barriers increase the number of imports that enter a country? .... 10. _____
11. Are governments allowed to restrict investments made by foreigners? .... 11. _____
12. Is profit usually the main reason why firms sell abroad? .... 12. _____
13. Does the WTO create and enforce rules governing trade within the United States? .... 13. _____
14. Does a trading bloc discourage free trade among its members? .... 14. _____
15. Is the IMF's main purpose to provide low-cost loans for roads and electric power plant development in less-developed countries? .... 15. _____
16. Do sales level off during the maturity stage of a product? .... 16. _____
17. Do American companies move to foreign countries when sales at home begin to grow? ... 17. _____
18. Does a balance of payments deficit exist when more money leaves a country than comes in? 18. _____
19. Might countries with prolonged trade deficits have to restrict the activities of foreign businesses in their countries? .... 19. _____
20. When the demand for foreign currency decreases, does the value of the dollar increase? ... 20. _____

Total Score _____

Part B—*Directions:* For each of the following statements, select the word, or group of words, that best completes the statement. In the Answers column, write the letter corresponding to the answer selected.

1. Which method is likely to be the least costly and risky way to expand abroad? (a) franchising, (b) licensing, (c) dumping, (d) exporting. .... 1._____

2. Two or more firms sharing the costs of doing business in foreign countries and also sharing the profits are (a) joint ventures, (b) strategic alliances, (c) wholly owned subsidiaries, (d) licensed enterprises. .... 2._____

3. If the United States sets a tariff of 15 percent on $150 cameras that are made in Germany, the cost of the camera in the United States will rise to (a) $155.50, (b) $165, (c) $172.50, (d) $175. .... 3._____

4. How do tariffs affect the prices of foreign goods? (a) Prices increase. (b) Prices decrease. (c) Prices remain the same. (d) Prices fluctuate at a quick pace. .... 4._____

5. Nontariff barriers (a) increase the number of imports that enter a country, (b) increase the value of one currency to another, (c) protect domestic producers, (d) protect foreign producers. .... 5._____

6. In a high-context culture such as Japan, communication would NOT likely be (a) direct, (b) gestures, (c) indirect, (d) vague. .... 6._____

7. If a U.S. company overproduces, the best way to dispose of its surplus goods profitably is to (a) advertise widely to attract buyers, (b) drop the price of the surplus goods to attract buyers, (c) create a trading bloc to create demand for the goods, (d) sell the surplus goods abroad. .... 7._____

8. In order to gain a trade advantage, a country specializes in a product it can provide more efficiently than can other countries. What theory is the country practicing? (a) balance of trade theory, (b) comparative advantage theory, (c) product life cycle theory, (d) balance of surplus theory. .... 8._____

9. The first two stages that a product goes through are the (a) introductory and growth stages, (b) introductory and decline stages, (c) growth and maturity stages, (d) growth and decline stages. .... 9._____

10. If the Canadians keep increasing the number of American cars purchased, (a) American products will become more expensive for Canadians, (b) Canadian products will become more expensive for Americans, (c) American products will become less expensive for Canadians, (d) Canadian products will become less expensive for Americans. .... 10._____

Total Score _____

Part C—*Directions:* In the Answers column, write the letter of the word or expression in Column I that most closely matches each statement in Column II.

Column I	Column II	Answers
A. culture	1. An example of a trading bloc	_____
B. dumping	2. Restrictions on quantities permitted to enter a country	_____
C. EU	3. Selling goods below cost in a foreign market	_____
D. exports	4. Goods and services purchased from other countries	_____
E. free trade	5. Customs, beliefs, values, and patterns of behavior of	
F. imports	the people of a country or group	_____
G. quotas	Total Score	_____

Directions: Study each controversial issue carefully. Follow the advice of your teacher before listing in the columns provided reasons why people might answer Yes or No. Your teacher may want you to work with a class-mate, talk with others in your community to gather information, or use the library or Internet to gather facts.

4-1. Should South America form a trading bloc that might be called SAFTA (South American Free Trade Association)?

Reasons for "Yes"	Reasons for "No"

4-2. Because of the growing importance of international trade and relations, should all students be required to study a foreign language and take a course dealing with world cultures?

Reasons for "Yes"	Reasons for "No"

PROBLEMS

4-A. Listed below are the names of ten of the world's largest firms. Use the library, the Internet, or other sources to name the home country and the main industry or product for each.

Company	Country	Industry
Aerospatiale	_____	_____
Bayer	_____	_____
Citizens Watch	_____	_____
E. I. DuPont de Nemours	_____	_____
Electrolux	_____	_____
Kia Motor	_____	_____
Northern Telecom	_____	_____
Petrofina	_____	_____
Siemens	_____	_____
Smithkline Beecham	_____	_____

4-B. Listed below is the value of exports shown in millions of dollars for three fictitious countries for selected products. Study the figures and answer the questions that follow.

	Galafo	Minion	Ungwa
Lumber	$1,350	$ 700	$ 0
Coffee	50	7,000	850
Rice	920	250	6,900
Fish	530	610	490

1. Which country is likely to have the competitive advantage for each of the following products?

   a. Lumber _____

   b. Coffee _____

   c. Rice _____

2. How could Galafo best trade with Minion?

   _____

   _____

   _____

3. How could Minion best trade with Ungwa?

   _____

   _____

   _____

4. If Ungwa had an embargo on Galafo's lumber, what might Ungwa do to obtain lumber?

   _____

   _____

   _____

   _____

   _____

4-C. Assume that the following chart shows the cost (in U.S. dollars) for selected products available to customers in four major world cities in a recent year. Study the chart and answer the questions below.

	New York	London	Tokyo	Mexico City
Compact disc	$ 12.99	$ 14.99	$ 22.09	$ 13.91
Movie	7.50	10.50	17.29	4.55
Sony Walkman (mid-range)	59.95	74.98	211.34	110.00
Cup of coffee	1.25	1.50	2.80	.91
Designer jeans	39.99	74.92	79.73	54.54
Nike Air Jordans	125.00	134.99	172.91	154.24

1. If you lived in Japan, which city would you most like to visit to get the best buys for your money?

_____

2. If you did not live in any of the countries represented by these cities, which city would you least like to visit if you decided to go on a shopping spree to buy some of the items listed above?

_____

3. What percentage more would an American pay for a movie in London than in New York?

_____

4. What percentage less would a New Yorker pay for a movie in Mexico City?

_____

5. What purchasing advice would you give to an American who wants to travel to London?

_____

_____

4-D. Indicate whether each situation described below is an embargo, tariff, quota, sanction, or nontariff barrier.

	Embargo	Tariff	Quota	Sanction	Nontariff Barrier
1. The United States limits the number of Japanese cars that may be imported each year.	____	____	____	____	____
2. The Japanese do not permit the importing of certain American products.	____	____	____	____	____
3. The U.S. government forbids U.S. companies from conducting business with Cuba.	____	____	____	____	____
4. France places a tax on alcoholic beverages imported from the United States.	____	____	____	____	____
5. Some countries do not buy VCRs from many producers because they are made mostly in black, which is the color of death.	____	____	____	____	____
6. The U.S. government might take this action if a foreign firm attempted to dump its products here.	____	____	____	____	____

4-E. Assume that the U.S. Department of Commerce reported the following figures on imports and exports of selected products in millions of dollars. Study the figures and answer the questions that follow.

	Exports	Imports
Coffee	$ 9.8	$ 1,735.6
Rice	752.2	80.3
Wheat	3,348.1	66.1
Clothing	3,211.6	26,205.8
Motorcycles/bicycles	1,302.6	1,635.9
Scientific instruments	13,487.6	6,757.4
Total	_____	_____

1. Calculate the total exports and imports and record each total in the space provided.

2. By how much did the imports exceed the exports? _____

3. Which goods are imported in greater quantity than exported? _____

4. Which goods are exported in greater quantity than imported? _____

5. Based on these products only, does a balance of trade surplus or deficit exist? _____

6. Which one item most contributed to the difference between the total imports and exports? _____

4-F. Assume that the following exchange rates for four countries equals one American dollar.

	Year 1	Year 2
Canadian dollar	1.28	1.37
French franc	5.69	5.56
Japanese yen	106	112
Mexican peso	3.35	3.13

1. Assume you bought the following products while vacationing over the last two years. Determine how much you paid in American dollars in the currency of the country you visited.

   a. Camera for 150 Canadian dollars (Year 1) _____

   b. Perfume for 110 French francs (Year 2) _____

   c. Jewelry for 50 Mexican pesos (Year 1) _____

2. Assume you bought binoculars in Japan in Year 1 for 8,700 yen and in Year 2 you returned to Japan for a second visit and you saw the item at the same store for 11,500 yen.

   a. In Year 1, what was the price for the binoculars in American dollars? _____

   b. What was the dollar price in Year 2? _____

4-G. Many countries belong to trading blocs. Place a check mark in the appropriate column to indicate whether the country is a member of the European Union (EU), North American Free Trade Association (NAFTA), or neither.

Country	EU	NAFTA	Neither
1. Greece	____	____	____
2. Britain	____	____	____
3. Mexico	____	____	____
4. Japan	____	____	____
5. Canada	____	____	____
6. Brazil	____	____	____
7. Italy	____	____	____

4-H. Assume that you have been working in an American company for several years and you now have the opportunity to work in one of its branch offices located in another country. Answer the following questions before you leave for your new job abroad.

1. Provide the name of the country to which you wish to be assigned. _____

2. Why did you select this country? _____

3. What is the currency, and how many units of that currency are equal to one American dollar?

   _____

4. Assume that your salary in the United States is $25,000 a year. What is it worth in the currency of your

   new country? _____

5. What are two main products that this country exports? _____

6. What are two main imports of this country? _____

7. What is the language of your new country? _____

8. Write the following sentence in the language of the country: "My name is . . . and I live in the United

   States of America." _____

   _____

9. What are the average temperatures for the following months:

   June _____   October _____

   January _____   March _____

10. Identify several different customs practiced in this country regarding such items as being on time for appointments, working hours, table etiquette, popular food dishes, eye contact, dress, holidays, and

    religion. _____

    _____

    _____

    _____

SMALL GROUP ACTIVITIES

Group Activity 1

Your instructor will place you into groups of two. With your partner, make a list of five nonbook items in your possession. Examples might include watches, jewelry, wallets/purses, sneakers, backpacks, pens, beepers, personal digital assistants, and cell phones. Next to each item, identify the country of origin. Report your results to the class.

After all pairs have reported their findings and recorded them on the board, the class should answer these questions together:

1. What are the top three countries identified?
2. How many countries in all are identified?
3. Which continents or regions of the world are most represented?
4. Are any particular industries more dominant than others? Which ones?

Group Activity 2

Find someone who recently came to this country from another country, either to live or as a visitor. Then ask that person the following questions and write notes summarizing the person's answers. Later you will be asked to share this information with your class.

1. When you first arrived in this country, what practices or behavior seemed most different from your country?
2. In your home country, if you need to tell someone on the job that you disagree with him or her, do you tell the person directly or do you only imply or hint that you disagree?
3. What time do people go to work on day jobs in your country and what time do they leave at the end of the day? How long is their lunch period? When do they have breaks during the day?
4. What is the procedure for obtaining a pay increase in your country when you believe you have earned it?
5. In your country, if you have been improperly treated or discriminated against on the job by your supervisor or other employees, would you have the right legally to sue your employer?
6. If an American went to your country, what things would you tell him or her to avoid doing?
7. How do you greet someone in person in your country and on the telephone? How do you say goodbye?

After obtaining answers to the above questions, your teacher will place you into groups based upon the language, country, or region of the world that you selected. Compare your answers with those of other members of your group to see whether your answers are similar or different. Your group should select a leader to report your results to the entire class.

Study Guide

Part A—*Directions:* Indicate your answer to each of the following questions by writing either yes or no in the Answers column.

Answers

1. Do most businesses start with several owners?... 1. _____
2. Is it typical for months and years to pass before a new business earns a profit?................. 2. _____
3. Do new businesses often fail for financial reasons? .... 3. _____
4. Do typical entrepreneurs give up quickly when they are not immediately successful?....... 4. _____
5. In recent years, have an increasing number of women opened their own businesses?......... 5. _____
6. Is the legal form of ownership one of the first decisions that a new owner must make? ..... 6. _____
7. Does the form of ownership selected depend upon the financial responsibility the owner is willing to assume? .... 7. _____
8. Should the entrepreneur write a business plan soon after launching the business?............. 8. _____
9. Is the corporation the most common form of ownership? .... 9. _____
10. Can as few as two people form a sole proprietorship?... 10. _____
11. Does it usually take less time for decisions to be made in a proprietorship than in other forms of business ownership? .... 11. _____
12. Can a sole proprietor be forced to use personal possessions to pay off debts if the business fails? .... 12. _____
13. Is a business that provides personal services well suited to the proprietorship form of organization? .... 13. _____
14. Is a partnership limited to a maximum of six partners? .... 14. _____
15. Can a partnership usually borrow money more readily than a sole proprietorship?............ 15. _____
16. If one person in a partnership is unable to pay business debts, are all other partners responsible for paying those debts? .... 16. _____
17. Is it true that a partner can lose only the amount of money invested in the partnership should the business fail? .... 17. _____
18. If a partner enters into a contract against the wishes of the other partners, are the other partners legally responsible for the contract?... 18. _____
19. Can the bankruptcy of any partner cause a sudden end to the partnership?....................... 19. _____
20. Must creditors be informed about the formation of a limited partnership? .... 20. _____

Total Score _____

Part B—*Directions:* For each of the following statements, select the word, or group of words, that best completes the statement. In the Answers column, write the letter corresponding to the answer selected.

1. New businesses mainly fail because (a) owners work short hours, (b) owners are too young, (c) owners lack financial resources, (d) owners would rather work for others. ....   1. _____

2. Which statement is true about successful entrepreneurs? (a) Most successful entrepreneurs experienced early successful startups. (b) Most successful entrepreneurs do not enjoy working on their own. (c) Most successful entrepreneurs feel that it is not necessary to obtain work experience in the types of businesses they launch. (d) Most successful entrepreneurs learned from their mistakes during unsuccessful startups and started over. ....   2. _____

3. To start your own business, you need (a) adequate funds; (b) adequate funds and a general knowledge about business; (c) adequate funds, a general knowledge about business, and some work experience; (d) adequate funds, a general knowledge about business, some work experience, and a business opportunity. ....   3. _____

4. The form of ownership selected depends upon (a) the capital needed and the financial responsibility the owner is willing to assume, (b) the nature and size of the business and the tax laws, (c) neither a nor b, (d) both a and b. ....   4. _____

5. The terms *capital, net worth,* and *equity* are (a) interchangeable and defined as assets less liabilities, (b) not interchangeable but defined as assets less liabilities, (c) interchangeable and defined as assets plus liabilities, (d) interchangeable and defined as assets plus capital.   5. _____

6. If a balance sheet shows cash as $118,000, liabilities as $115,000, and capital as $125,000, how much would the noncash assets be worth? (a) $122,000, (b) $233,000, (c) $240,000, (d) $243,000. ....   6. _____

7. Approximately how many businesses are formed as proprietorships? (a) one out of two, (b) two out of three, (c) three out of four, (d) four out of five. ....   7. _____

8. Which statement is true about proprietorships? (a) The owner must consult with others before making decisions. (b) The owner pays less income tax than corporations. (c) The owner shares all losses. (d) The owner shares all profits. ....   8. _____

9. If one partner makes a contract that the other partners do not like, (a) only the partner making the contract is bound by it, (b) all partners are bound by it, (c) only the agreeing partners are bound by it, (d) the other partners can reject the contract. ....   9. _____

10. The trade name of a business (a) does not reduce the owners' liability to creditors, (b) cannot be an artificial name, (c) cannot be listed as the Dixie Service Company, (d) does not have to be registered. ....   10. _____

Total Score   _____

Part C—*Directions:* Below are descriptions of several types of business firms. Indicate which form of business ownership would be best for each business by placing a check mark in the appropriate column.

Description	Proprietorship	Partnership
1. The owner of a small grocery store wants to expand but does not have the capital.	_____	_____
2. An accountant is opening an office in a small town.	_____	_____
3. A farmer wants to sell fruits and vegetables from a roadside stand.	_____	_____
4. A person who has worked as a repairer of large appliances wants to open a store to sell and service appliances. The person has had no experience in sales.	_____	_____
5. A person who will be retiring in ten years wants an employee to begin taking over the business.	_____	_____

Total Score   _____

Directions: Study each controversial issue carefully. Follow the advice of your teacher before listing in the columns provided reasons why people might answer Yes or No. Your teacher may want you to work with a classmate, talk with others in your community to gather information, or use the library or Internet to gather facts.

5-1. Should states pass requirements, such as reaching a minimum age of 21 or obtaining a license, that individuals must meet in order to form a partnership?

Reasons for "Yes"	Reasons for "No"

5-2. In a partnership of three or more people, should all major decisions require only a majority vote of the partners?

Reasons for "Yes"	Reasons for "No"

PROBLEMS

5-A. Below are statements about entrepreneurs.

a. Read each statement and indicate whether you agree or disagree.

b. Ask two adults to answer these same statements.

c. Decide whether you would change any of your answers based on the responses of the adults you talked to. Then ask your teacher for the results of a study of entrepreneurs.

		Agree	Disagree
1.	Entrepreneurs are most commonly the oldest children in their families.	_____	_____
2.	The large majority of entrepreneurs are married.	_____	_____
3.	Three out of four entrepreneurs have college degrees.	_____	_____
4.	The primary reason entrepreneurs start their own businesses is that they don't like working for others.	_____	_____
5.	Entrepreneurs are risk takers but not high-risk takers.	_____	_____
6.	The majority of entrepreneurs are from families where one or both parents were at one time entrepreneurs.	_____	_____

5-B. Prospective business owners should make a business plan before starting the business. The plan is usually divided into the sections shown below. Study each of the following statements from a business plan and indicate in which section of the plan it would best belong.

Section I:	Nature of the Business
Section II:	Goals and Objectives
Section III:	Marketing Plan
Section IV:	Financial Plan
Section V:	Organizational Plan

1. "Money from my savings accounts and from an uncle—amounting to $9,000—will be used to launch the business." _____

2. "By the end of one year, I plan to make no profit nor do I expect to incur any losses; but by the end of the second year, I expect to make a net profit of $8,000." _____

3. "My oldest brother, Tom, will handle the marketing and hiring of workers, and I will handle the buying of merchandise and all money matters." _____

4. "The business will be located at 19 Chestnut Street, which should be a good location in relation to competitive businesses." _____

5-C. In 1981, John Sortino started selling teddy bears from a cart in downtown Burlington, Vermont. He made them of high-quality materials and did reasonably well. He later added two partners to his growing business. Because most teddy bears are sold from stores for children, John wanted to distinguish his bears from the store-bought bears. He decided to gift wrap and personalize the bears in order to appeal to people of all ages. He also mailed them as gifts for special occasions, including birthdays and promotions. The idea of Bear-Grams caught on quickly. Ten years later, sales were $18 million. Sales doubled each year. Because the Vermont Teddy Bear Company does not operate in many states, growth opportunities are still great.

1. Assuming growth continued at the same rate, what dollar sales were received in the eleventh year?

_____

2. Many of Vermont Teddy Bear Company's customers order from outside of Burlington. How do you think

the company attracts its many customers? _____

3. Name four special occasions when someone might send a Bear-Gram.

_____

_____

_____

_____

4. Some of the employees recommended that to fulfill the firm's social responsibility, it should donate Bear-

Grams to certain people or groups. What types of people or groups would you recommend donating the

bears to if you were an employee? _____

_____

5-D. Owning a business as a proprietorship offers several advantages to the owner. However, there are also many advantages of partnerships. For each of the items listed, indicate whether it is an advantage of a proprietorship or a partnership by placing a check mark in the appropriate column.

	Proprietorship	Partnership
1. The owner has sole claim to the assets of the business.	_____	_____
2. An individual is bound only to those contracts he or she has made. ...	_____	_____
3. The management skills of more than one person are combined.	_____	_____
4. Money needed for business operations is easier to obtain.	_____	_____
5. An owner can more easily retire from management and keep the business operating.	_____	_____
6. The management of the business is more flexible.	_____	_____
7. If losses occur, one owner does not usually have to pay the entire amount.	_____	_____
8. It is very easy to begin and end the business.	_____	_____
9. Employees understand clearly where final responsibility and authority are located.	_____	_____
10. Decisions about business problems are easier to make.	_____	_____

5-E. Below are listed possible businesses that one might consider starting. For each business, indicate whether you might be interested in it. Give reasons for your answers.

1. Physical fitness and tennis center _____

   _____

2. Personal shopping service for people who are too busy to do their own shopping _____

   _____

3. Fresh flowers and plant shop _____

   _____

4. Recycled music store selling used records, cassette tapes, and compact discs _____

   _____

5-F. Read the following case situation and answer the questions that follow.

Drs. Johnson, Jenson, and Jacobi formed a medical services partnership. Dr. Johnson is an eye specialist, Dr. Jenson is a nose specialist, and Dr. Jacobi specializes in ear surgery. Each contributed an equal amount of capital to open the business and orally agreed to divide all profits equally. Two office workers and three medical assistants were hired. A meeting is held each month to discuss business matters and to make decisions.

Within a year, their medical practice was doing quite well. However, problems arose. There was much confusion in scheduling patients, paying bills, and dividing earnings. The office staff seemed to spend much more time doing Dr. Jenson's paperwork than anyone else's. Dr. Jacobi generated far more income than Drs. Johnson and Jenson. As a result, Dr. Jacobi felt he should receive more of the profits than Drs. Johnson and Jenson. The nurses also believed they should be paid more for their services and overtime.

1. In the absence of a written partnership agreement, what percent of the profits should each partner receive

   according to the law? _____

   _____

   _____

   _____

2. If the partners were to decide to write a partnership agreement, what problem will be the most difficult to agree

   upon? _____

   _____

   _____

   _____

3. Assume that the three doctors decided that after all expenses are paid each year, the profits will be divided

   as follows: Dr. Johnson, 30%; Dr. Jenson, 30%; and Dr. Jacobi, 40%. For the year just ended, the profits

   were $350,000. How much will each partner receive when the profits are distributed?

   a. Dr. Johnson: _____

   b. Dr. Jenson: _____

   c. Dr. Jacobi: _____

5-G. Thomas W. Henry and Marie T. Shaw decide to form a partnership on November 1 of the current year for the purpose of operating a business that will repair electronic equipment such as televisions and DVD players. Henry will invest $40,000 and Shaw, $30,000. The business will be located at 640 Main Street, Centerville, New York, and will be known as the Frontier Television Shop. The partnership is to run for five years. Henry is to have general supervision of television repairs, and Shaw is to be in charge of all other electronic repairs. Each partner will draw a monthly salary of $2,000. Profits are to be shared in proportion to the investments of the partners.

Using the information given above, fill in the partnership agreement form that follows.

Partnership Agreement

THIS CONTRACT, Made and entered into on the day of (1.) _____ of (2.) 20 _____ by and between (3.)

_____

WITNESSES: That the said parties have this day formed a partnership for the purpose of engaging in and conducting (4.)

_____

under the following stipulations, which are made a part of the contract:

FIRST: The said partnership is to continue for a term of (5.) _____ from date hereof.

SECOND: The business shall be conducted under the firm name of (6.)

_____ at (7.) _____

THIRD: The investments are as follows: (8.) _____

_____

FOURTH: All profits or losses arising from said business are to be divided as follows: (9.)

_____

_____

FIFTH: Each partner is to devote his or her entire time and attention to the business and to engage in no other business enterprise without the written consent of the other.

SIXTH: Each partner is to have a salary of (10.) $ _____ a month, the same to be withdrawn at such time or times as he or she may elect. Neither partner is to withdraw from the business an amount in excess of his or her salary without the written consent of the other.

SEVENTH: The duties of each partner are defined as follows. (11.)

_____

_____

EIGHTH: Neither partner is to become surety or bondsperson for anyone without the written consent of the other.

NINTH: (12.) _____

TENTH: (13.) _____

IN WITNESS WHEREOF, The parties aforesaid have hereunto set their hands and affixed their seals on the day and year above written.

(14.) _____

(15.) _____

5-H. Answer the following questions about the partnership of Thomas Henry and Marie Shaw in Problem 5-G:

1. After the salaries to the partners have been paid, the profits for a particular year amounted to $37,800.

    Henry's share will be: _____ .   Shaw's share will be: _____.

2. Since Henry has the larger investment in the partnership, does he have more authority than Shaw in decid-

    ing how to operate the business? _____

3. Without Shaw's knowledge, Henry placed an order for ten television sets of a new make. Will the partner-

    ship be bound by this contract? _____

4. Is the partnership operating under a trade name? _____

5. Can the partnership be dissolved before the end of five years by mutual agreement of the two partners?

    _____

SMALL GROUP ACTIVITIES

Group Activity 1

Your teacher will divide the class into groups of three to five students. Each group member is to select a small business—a sole proprietorship—and interview the entrepreneur. Ask the following questions:

1. Before starting your business, did you prepare a business plan? If yes, did you spend much time developing the plan?

   _____

   _____

2. If you needed to obtain a loan, did your bank or other lenders examine the business plan?

   _____

   _____

3. Did you own a business prior to this one? If so, what kind?

   _____

   _____

4. What were your biggest worries when you first got started?

   _____

   _____

5. Are your customers of the type you expected to attract?

   _____

   _____

6. Do you plan to enlarge your business, move to a new location, or open a new branch?

   _____

   _____

7. If you were to expand your business, would you form a partnership or a corporation?

   _____

   _____

8. If you could start your business over again, what would you do differently?

   _____

   _____

9. What do you like most and least about being an entrepreneur?

   _____

   _____

10. What advice would you give to a young person wanting to become an entrepreneur?

    _____

    _____

After all group members finish their interviews, the group should meet to share their answers. Your group should then prepare a brief written summary of the three to five businesses represented and make a report to your class.

Group Activity 2

Your teacher will assign you to a three-person group of students, and your group will operate a new partnership. Your business sells outdoor furniture in a small southern city in the United States. Your products include such items as patio chairs, tables, and umbrellas. You and your two partners made an equal investment to get the business started. One of you has training and experience in marketing, another in accounting, and the third in managing people. Each person, however, is able to fill in for the others during busy times.

During your first year of operations, the problems listed below arise, and you and your partners need to agree on solutions. You must discuss and resolve each of the situations. Note your group's decisions and report them to the class.

1. At the outset, the business needs a name that reflects the nature of the business.

   _____

2. The partners need to be assigned job responsibilities and titles.

   _____

3. Everyone agrees that the business should be open at least 6 1/2 days a week. The weekday hours approved by all are Monday through Friday, 10:00 a.m. until 6:00 p.m.; Saturdays, 10:00 a.m. until 8:00 p.m.; and Sundays, 1:00 p.m. until 5:00 p.m. A big argument arises over who should work what days and hours. No one seems to want to work on weekends.

   _____

   _____

4. One partner calculates that he/she works, on average, eight hours per week more than the other two partners and demands that his/her share of the profits be increased by 20 percent. This partner is single, and the two other partners are married with young children.

   _____

   _____

5. The new business does quite well for the first half of the year, and then sales start to decline. The business is not making enough money to satisfy one of the partners, who suggests that the business be dissolved before everyone "loses their shirts." The second partner disagrees, saying, "It takes time to build our reputation." The third partner is undecided.

   _____

   _____

Study Guide

Part A—*Directions:* Indicate your answer to each of the following questions by writing either yes or no in the Answers column.

Answers

1. Although a corporation is owned by a group of people, does it act as if it were a single person? .... 1. _____
2. Is a corporation allowed to make contracts but not borrow money? .... 2. _____
3. Is it possible for a corporation to be sued in its own name? .... 3. _____
4. Can a person who buys only one share of stock become an owner of a corporation? .... 4. _____
5. Is a dividend the amount of money a person pays to buy a share of stock? .... 5. _____
6. Could a stockholder be responsible for all the debts of a corporation? .... 6. _____
7. Can creditors collect from stockholders if the corporation fails? .... 7. _____
8. Are the members of the board of directors elected by stockholders? .... 8. _____
9. Can a corporation make important changes in the purpose of its business without changing its charter? .... 9. _____
10. When shares are transferred, must the transfer of ownership be indicated in the records of the corporation? .... 10. _____
11. Is the annual state tax rate for corporations based on profits? .... 11. _____
12. Is it possible for some corporations to avoid double taxation? .... 12. _____
13. Does a joint venture occur when two major contractors agree to connect two cities by building a tunnel under a river? .... 13. _____
14. Do virtual corporations tend to be temporary relationships? .... 14. _____
15. Does a cooperative provide members with both cost and profit advantages that they would not have individually? .... 15. _____
16. Is a limited liability company taxed as if it were a sole proprietorship or partnership? ...... 16. _____
17. Is a major strength of an LLC its limited liability feature? .... 17. _____
18. Do large corporations and multinational firms usually qualify as LLCs? .... 18. _____
19. Does a nonprofit corporation pay dividends to shareholders? .... 19. _____
20. Is a "quasi-public corporation" operated only by state governments? .... 20. _____

Total Score _____

Part B—*Directions:* For each of the following statements, select the word, or group of words, that best completes the statement. In the Answers column, write the letter corresponding to the answer selected.

1. Corporations tend to be (a) many in number and small in size, (b) many in number and large in size, (c) few in number and large in size, (d) few in number and small in size. .....   1. _____

2. In a recent year, corporate sales of goods and services were about (a) four times more than sales from partnerships, (b) eight times more than sales from partnerships, (c) twelve times more than sales from partnerships, (d) sixteen times more than sales from partnerships.   2. _____

3. An official document giving power to run a corporation is a (a) stock certificate, (b) charter, (c) proxy, (d) shareholder certificate. ....   3. _____

4. Shareholders of a corporation are often called (a) boards, (b) officers, (c) owners, (d) buyers.   4. _____

5. Net proceeds refer to the (a) cash received from the sale of all assets, (b) accumulation of capital, (c) payment of all debts, (d) cash received from the sale of all assets minus the payments of all debts. ....   5. _____

6. Unissued shares are the (a) shares bought by the organizers, (b) shares bought by the shareholders, (c) shares that might be sold and used to expand the business at a later date, (d) shares bought by the board of directors. ....   6. _____

7. Which statement is true about obtaining money in corporations? (a) Corporations have a more difficult time than proprietorships in raising capital. (b) Partnerships have an easier time raising money than do corporations. (c) Corporations can borrow money more easily than can partnerships. (d) Proprietorships and partnerships have an easier time raising money than do corporations. ....   7. _____

8. People who invest in a corporation are (a) legally liable for the debts of the corporation beyond their investment in the shares purchased, (b) not taxed on dividends received, (c) provided one vote regardless of the number of shares held, (d) financially liable up to the amount originally invested. ....   8. _____

9. When an owner of a corporation dies, (a) the business automatically ends, (b) the corporation must be changed to either a partnership or a sole proprietorship, (c) the life of the corporation is not affected, (d) the corporation must be changed to a closely held corporation.   9. _____

10. Taxes that are unique to a corporation are (a) a filing fee for a charter and an organization tax; (b) a filing fee and an annual state tax; (c) a filing fee, an organization tax, and an annual state tax; (d) a filing fee, an organization tax, an annual state tax, and a federal income tax. ....   10. _____

11. A corporation with taxable earnings of $74,000 has a tax rate of 15% on the first $50,000 and a 25% tax rate on the next $25,000. The federal income taxes will amount to (a) $13,500, (b) $17,100, (c) $18,500, (d) $29,600. ....   11. _____

12. An agreement that involves two or more businesses to provide a good or service is called (a) a corporation, (b) a joint venture, (c) a nonprofit organization, (d) an LLC. ....   12. _____

13. A virtual corporation (a) is not a form of joint venture, (b) does not include business partners who are competitors, (c) takes advantage of fast-changing market conditions, (d) operates solely on its own to take advantage of special opportunities. ....   13. _____

14. In order to form a Subchapter S corporation, what is the maximum number of stockholders that the firm can have? (a) 5, (b) 15, (c) 25, (d) 100. ....   14. _____

15. The Tennessee Valley Authority is an example of a (a) close corporation, (b) open corporation, (c) quasi-public corporation, (d) virtual corporation. ....   15. _____

Total Score   _____

Chapter 6: Controversial Issues   Name _____

Directions: Study each controversial issue carefully. Follow the advice of your teacher before listing in the columns provided reasons why people might answer Yes or No. Your teacher may want you to work with a classmate, talk with others in your community to gather information, or use the library or Internet to gather facts.

6-1. Because many small stockholders do not cast their proxy ballots, should corporations be permitted to sell common stock without voting privileges at a somewhat lower price?

Reasons for "Yes"	Reasons for "No"

6-2. Should the dividends paid to stockholders of corporations be taxed by the federal government?

Reasons for "Yes"	Reasons for "No"

PROBLEMS

6-A. Corporations have to meet many more legal requirements than proprietorships or partnerships. The following list describes activities of a corporation. Write the letter *L* after those activities that are legal; write the letter *N* after those activities that are NOT usually legal.

1. Three people start a corporation without obtaining approval of the state in which it will operate. _____

2. A person who is not a shareholder is elected to the board of directors. _____

3. An open corporation allows only relatives of current owners to buy its stock. _____

4. After receiving permission to do business from only one state, the corporation operates in ten other states. _____

5. A stockholder is sued by creditors for personal assets beyond the amount of the original investment. _____

6. Everyone who has *ever* owned stock in the company is allowed to vote at the annual meeting. _____

7. The name of the corporation is Tot Toy Company, Inc. _____

8. Dividends are given only to the shareholders owning the most stock. _____

9. Shareholders are required to pay taxes on the dividends they receive. _____

10. One shareholder signs an authorization for the president of the corporation to cast the stockholder's vote at the annual meeting. _____

6-B. Assume there are 13.7 million proprietorships, 1.7 million partnerships, and 3.6 million corporations in the United States. However, corporations sell 90 percent of all goods and services. Proprietorships sell 6 percent, and partnerships sell 4 percent. (*With your teacher's permission, the following activities may also be completed on a computer.*)

1. In the circle below on the left, construct a pie chart to show the percentage of businesses by the type of ownership.
2. In the circle below on the right, construct a pie chart to show the percentage of sales by the type of ownership.

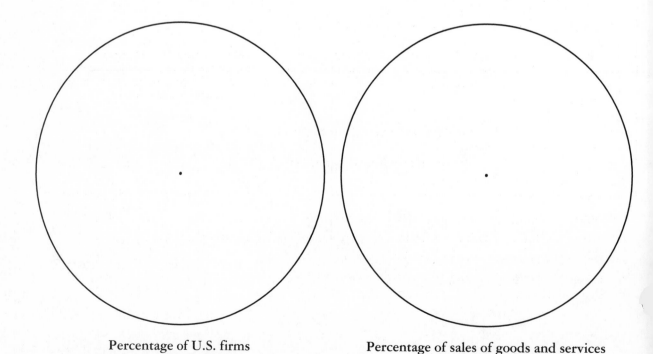

Percentage of U.S. firms by type of ownership	Percentage of sales of goods and services by type of ownership

3. What conclusions can you make from the two charts?

_____

_____

_____

6-C. Which of the following statements are rights of stockholders and which are not?

	Rights of Stockholders	Not a Right of Stockholders
1. To sell shares to other stockholders..	_____	_____
2. To vote for members of the board of directors...........................	_____	_____
3. To vote on who is hired as president..	_____	_____
4. To work as a manager in the corporation	_____	_____
5. To receive notices of stockholders' meetings...........................	_____	_____
6. To vote on certain matters even if they cannot be present at stockholders' meetings..	_____	_____
7. To attend all meetings of the board of directors.......................	_____	_____

6-D. Study the following proxy and the accompanying explanatory notes that appear in the notice of the annual stockholders' meeting. Then complete the five activities that follow by recording your answers on the proxy.

XYZ CORP.

Proxy No.

```
0   067 515
☐00000
11111☐1
2222222
3333333
4444444
5555☐5☐
66☐6666
777☐777
8888888
9999999
```

XYZ's directors recommend a vote for the proposals numbered 1 and 2 and against the stockholder proposals numbered 3 and 4 and SHARES WILL BE SO VOTED UNLESS OTHERWISE INDICATED:

1. FOR ☐ NOT FOR ☐ election of directors
J. Smith, M. Jones, T. Benson, R. Juarez,
A. Bonini, C. Jackson
(*To withhold authority to vote for any individual nominee, strike out that nominee's name.*)

2. FOR ☐ AGAINST ☐ ABSTAIN ☐
Ratify appointment of Chen Accounting Inc. as auditing firm.

3. FOR ☐ AGAINST ☐ ABSTAIN ☐
Approve the authorization of 100,000 shares of preferred stock.

4. FOR ☐ AGAINST ☐ ABSTAIN ☐
Stockholder proposal to outlaw the use of live animals to conduct research that may lead to future company profits.

X _____
PLEASE SIGN HERE AND RETURN PROMPTLY
Dated:
☐ Please send me a ticket for the St. Louis meeting

---

1. Vote for all board of director nominees, except M. Jones.
2. Vote as the directors wish you to do for Chen Accounting Inc. as the auditing firm.
3. Vote as you personally desire for stockholder proposal No. 3.
4. Vote as you personally desire for stockholder proposal No. 4.
5. Sign and date the proxy.

6-E. A small corporation has calculated its taxable earnings for the year to be $120,000. Complete the table below to determine the total income taxes the corporation will pay.

	Tax Rate	Tax
Not over $50,000	15%	_____
Over $50,000, but not over $75,000	25%	_____
Over $75,000, but not over $100,000	34%	_____
Over $100,000, but not over $335,000	39%	_____
TOTAL TAX		_____

6-F. For each of the items below, indicate by letter in the space provided which of the following types of organizational structures is most suitable.

A. Cooperative   D. Nonprofit Corporation
B. Corporation   E. Limited Liability Company (LLC)
C. Joint Venture   F. Virtual Corporation

___ 1. Three people who own a partnership wish to convert to some other type of structure that would limit their liability.

___ 2. Twenty partners from three different countries run a highly successful partnership and need an extremely large amount of capital in order to expand.

___ 3. Fifteen separate growers of cranberries located near each other meet regularly to discuss ways to improve growing and harvesting methods and now decide they wish to form a group that would handle sales of their product.

___ 4. Three small competitors individually see an opportunity to produce and sell a new product, but they must move quickly to succeed over larger competitors. None of them alone have the resources or expertise, but combined they do.

6-G. Study the table below and answer the questions that follow.

Some Top Farm Cooperatives	Products	Annual Sales (in millions)	Percent of Total Sales
Land O'Lakes	Butter & Dairy Products	$7,600	_____
Ocean Spray	Cranberry Juice & Products	1,400	_____
Sunkist	Citrus Fruits	1,005	_____
Blue Diamond	Almonds & Other Nuts	675	_____
Welch's	Grape Juice	600	_____
TOTAL		_____	

1. Calculate the total annual sales for the five farm cooperatives. Record your answer above.

2. Determine the percent of total sales for each company. Record your answers above.

3. If the two companies that produce juice were to merge, what percent of the total sales would they possess?

_____

6-H. After reading this case problem, answer the questions that follow.

The Snorkel Company was operated as a partnership for years by Ann Bird, Pat Rossi, and Ron Shaffer. Primarily to gain additional capital, they converted their partnership to a corporation. It then became known as Snorkel Company, Inc. Five friends invested large sums of money by buying shares of stock in the new corporation. The company remained a close corporation.

All eight shareholders were extremely satisfied with the profits for the corporation's first five years. But, as the firm has continued to improve its profits, the owners have become more upset. Ron Shaffer summed up the feelings of everyone when he said, "This double taxation is killing me." The eight shareholders have become so distressed that they are seriously thinking about reorganizing again into a partnership.

1. Why was the "*Inc.*" added to the title of the company?

   _____

   _____

2. What did Ron Shaffer mean by "double taxation"?

   _____

   _____

   _____

3. Explain how the company can avoid double taxation without going back to being a partnership.

   _____

   _____

   _____

   _____

6-I. The following chart describes several stock purchases and the dividends paid on those stocks. Fill in the missing values for each stock purchase to complete the chart. The first row has been completed as an example.

Number of Shares	Price per Share	Total Cost	Dividends per Share	Total Dividends	Total Dividends as a Percent of Total Cost (to nearest whole percent)
350	$26.00	$ 9,100.00	$1.25	$ 437.50	5%
125		437.50	0.50		
	10.50	2,100.00			10%
670	56.00			2,251.20	
20		675.00	0.80		
	45.00	2,925.00			13%

SMALL GROUP ACTIVITIES

Group Activity 1

Your instructor will place you into groups of three to five students for the purpose of forming a small corporation. Each member will invest $10,000. Your group tasks are to complete the three phases below.

Phase 1: Getting Started

1. Decide on what type of small corporation to form in your area.
2. State the general purpose of your corporation and the type of product or service you will provide.
3. Identify the type or types of customers you wish to serve.
4. List specific means by which you can promote your goods or services to your customers.
5. Determine which student members will serve as CEO, Vice President, and Secretary and Treasurer.

Phase 2: Getting Incorporated

6. Prepare a Certificate of Incorporation—see Figure 6-1 in your textbook.
7. Prepare a simple financial plan and a balance sheet.
8. Learn from library or Internet materials the procedures for incorporating a business.
9. Ask an attorney for incorporation papers, for an estimate of the time needed to incorporate, and for an estimate of the state and attorney's costs for forming a small corporation.

Phase 3: Reporting Results

10. Your group should prepare a report for the class that your officers will present.
11. After each officer reports to the class about the group's corporation, other class members may ask questions.

Group Activity 2

This activity is a question-answering game. Students will write questions and answer questions in groups. Here are the rules:

1. All students are to write five or more one-sentence questions in the time allowed that are based upon the material in the chapter. Answers may be yes-no, true-false, or a few words. Next to each question, write the answer and the text page number where the answer can be found.
2. Your teacher will then place the class into groups of three students each. An even number of teams is required. If there are students remaining, each can join a different team of three. Each group will review the questions their members created. The group will select the 16 best questions, revising any that might need to be more clearly written.
3. Your teacher will select two teams to start the contest. One team asks the other team four questions and then decides whether the answers are correct. The teacher serves as the judge and handles disputes. The other team then poses four of its questions to the first team. For each correct answer, the answering team earns two points. If the question is not sufficiently clear, as decided by the teacher, the asking team loses two points. (Only one answer is allowed; no second guesses. The points can be recorded on the board.)
4. When both teams have completed asking and answering their four questions, the scores are added, and the team with the most points wins. If there is a tie, each team can ask another question until the tie is broken.
5. Two more teams now compete in the same manner as the first two teams until a winner is identified. This process should continue until all teams have competed.
6. The winning teams are now paired and compete against each other. The process continues until there is one final winner.

Study Guide

Part A—*Directions:* Indicate your answer to each of the following questions by writing either yes or no in the Answers column.

Answers

1. Does a monopoly exist as long as there are at least two producers? .... 1. _____
2. When competition exists, are prices generally higher than when a monopoly exists? .... 2. _____
3. Does competitive pricing cause less efficient companies to struggle for survival? .... 3. _____
4. Does the Sherman Antitrust Act permit competitors to agree to set the same selling prices on goods? .... 4. _____
5. Under the Clayton Act, can a business that produces computers require a buyer to also purchase supplies, such as paper and toner that are needed to run the computer? .... 5. _____
6. Can owners of a firm get protection by filing for bankruptcy? .... 6. _____
7. Do unpaid debts of a bankrupt firm stay on file for ten years? .... 7. _____
8. Can a firm that filed for bankruptcy obtain credit easily for new startups? .... 8. _____
9. Is it generally lawful to publish work that is protected by a copyright without permission of the author or publisher? .... 9. _____
10. Is it illegal to copy computer programs to distribute to friends? .... 10. _____
11. Is a trademark a type of monopoly? .... 11. _____
12. Does research show that the majority of those who smoke when young die prematurely of smoking-related diseases? .... 12. _____
13. Under the federal Warranty Act, must sellers specify what they will or will not do if their product is defective? .... 13. _____
14. If a customer is refused a loan because a store gave an incorrect credit balance to a bank, are both the store that provided the incorrect information and the bank that refused credit liable? .... 14. _____
15. Is it a crime for any unauthorized person to access a major computer system and view, use, or change data? .... 15. _____
16. Does the federal government regulate interstate as well as intrastate commerce? .... 16. _____
17. Do state and local governments use licensing to limit and control the number of certain types of businesses? .... 17. _____
18. Is it possible to both copyright and license a software program? .... 18. _____
19. Is a progressive tax a single tax rate that is the same for everyone? .... 19. _____
20. Because a sales tax applies to purchases rather than to income, is it a regressive tax? .... 20. _____

Total Score _____

Part B—*Directions:* For each of the following statements, select the word, or group of words, that best completes the statement. In the Answers column, write the letter corresponding to the answer selected.

Answers

1. What is the name of the 1936 act whose main purpose was to prevent setting different prices for different customers? (a) Clayton Act, (b) Robinson-Patman Act, (c) Sherman Antitrust Act, (d) Wheeler-Lea Act. .... 1. _____

2. Which act included outlawing unfair practices such as false advertising? (a) Clayton Act, (b) Robinson-Patman Act, (c) Sherman Antitrust Act, (d) Wheeler-Lea Act. .... 2. _____

3. Which practice allows a business to sell its assets to pay it debts? (a) licensing, (b) zoning, (c) bankruptcy, (d) monopoly. .... 3. _____

4. Once a business files for bankruptcy, under the law, (a) it must close its doors immediately, (b) it must close its doors within a six-month period, (c) it can continue to operate for a few months until it sells its assets, (d) it can create a survival plan that might enable it to recover. .... 4. _____

5. Which of the following is NOT an illegal practice? (a) copying tapes and programs for distribution to others, (b) copying an employer's software program for personal use on a home computer, (c) using another firm's trademark to promote a product, (d) photocopying a copyrighted article for distribution in a classroom. .... 5. _____

6. Under a federal Warranty Act, (a) sellers cannot set different prices for different customers, (b) cosmetic producers must show products will not be harmful when used, (c) sellers must specify what they will or will not do if their product is defective, (d) consumers cannot sue manufacturers. .... 6. _____

7. A policy of taxation based on one's ability to pay is called (a) proportional taxation, (b) progressive taxation, (c) regressive taxation, (d) flat taxation. .... 7. _____

8. A tax that is levied on the profits of businesses and on earnings of individuals is (a) a sales tax, (b) a federal excise tax, (c) an income tax, (d) a property tax. .... 8. _____

9. The largest source of revenue for the federal government is the (a) sales tax, (b) income tax, (c) property tax, (d) progressive tax. .... 9. _____

10. The main source of revenue for most local governments is the (a) property tax, (b) sales tax, (c) income tax, (d) assessed tax. .... 10. _____

Total Score _____

Part C—*Directions:* In the Answers column, write the letter of the word or expression in Column I that most closely matches each statement in Column II.

Column I	Column II	Answers
A. Copyright Office	1. Protects creators of software, novels, histories, poetry, and textbooks.	_____
B. Federal Communications Commission	2. Regulates stocks and bonds.	_____
C. Food and Drug Administration	3. Enforces laws dealing with unfair competition. ...	_____
D. Federal Power Commission	4. Regulates radio, television, telephone, and satellite communications.	_____
E. Federal Trade Commission	5. Grants property rights to inventors.	_____
F. Securities and Exchange Commission		
G. Patent and Trademark Office	Total Score	_____

Directions: Study each controversial issue carefully. Follow the advice of your teacher before listing in the columns provided reasons why people might answer Yes or No. Your teacher may want you to work with a classmate, talk with others in your community to gather information, or use the library or Internet to gather facts.

7-1. Should a federal law be passed that would prevent all organizations that collect information about individuals from selling or sharing that information with anyone else without the individuals' written approval?

Reasons for "Yes"	Reasons for "No"

7-2. Should the federal government substantially raise the so-called "sin taxes" on tobacco products and alcoholic beverages to increase federal revenues and to discourage the use of these products?

Reasons for "Yes"	Reasons for "No"

PROBLEMS

7-A. Place a check mark in the column at the right by the types of businesses that would most likely meet the qualifications for being considered a monopoly.

1. Automobile manufacturing business   _____
2. Gas utility company   _____
3. Nuclear power generation plant   _____
4. Cosmetic development laboratory   _____
5. Computer production plant   _____

7-B. Write the name of the main federal law that regulates each of the following business practices.

1. Prevents two competitors from agreeing to set the same prices in order that both might do well financially.

   _____

2. Forbids specifying goods that a buyer must purchase in order to get other goods.

   _____

3. Outlaws false advertising.

   _____

4. Stops competitors from charging different prices to different customers.

   _____

5. Prohibits the sale of unhealthful products that people eat, take as medicine, or apply to their bodies.

   _____

6. Stops businesses from selling non-food products that are found to be dangerous when used.

   _____

7-C. Study each business practice listed below, and place a check mark in the column at the right if the practice is prohibited by the Federal Trade Commission.

1. Putting "Made in the U.S.A." on a product that was made in South Korea. ....   _____
2. Selling as "new" undamaged car parts that were obtained by buying late-model wrecked cars and removing undamaged parts. ....   _____
3. A bookstore that does not regularly sell pens advertises in a local newspaper: "A free pen when you buy two or more books." ....   _____
4. A small, new store uses a well-known trademark of a large, famous store. ....   _____
5. A store sells jeans at the regular price, despite running a newspaper ad stating, "Big discounts on new designer jeans." ....   _____
6. A store runs a newspaper ad stating, "50% discount on all small appliances in our downtown store only, but not in any of our five suburban branches." ....   _____

7-D. Read the following article prepared by a government agency that regulates business activity, and answer the following questions.

Look for That Label*

"Hey, mister, wanna buy a genuine seal fur coat for your wife? A real bargain. Look at the label—the real McCoy. Only $500. But, you gotta buy now."

If anyone approaches you with a deal like this—BEWARE! You may be taken in by a fly-by-night operator. He or she has a label on the fur—but not a legal one. WHAT'S THIS ABOUT A LABEL?

When you buy a garment, a fur, or a fabric in a store, it often carries a label telling who made it or from which store it was purchased.

More important is the label that is attached to a wool, fur, or textile product that tells you of what the product is made.

This label is required by law. It should be written in plain English and be where you can find it easily. Either on or close to the label should be the name of the one responsible for the label's truth (either the person's name or code number, which is registered with the FTC).

Most shoppers today aren't expert enough to know exactly what kind of fur or material they buy. So, they must put their faith in the store that sells the product or in what the label says.

To be absolutely sure of what you buy, you would need a chemical laboratory and a microscope, and you would have to go through much training to learn to examine the fur or material to know the truth.

Congress passed laws assuring the consuming public it would get the kind of furs and textiles for which it paid.

The Federal Trade Commission was given the job of enforcing the laws. It is a tremendous task—one that would be far beyond the capacity of the FTC except for the fact that most sellers of these products are willing to abide by the laws.

Source: Adapted from FTC Buyer's Guide No. 6, "Look for That Label"

1. For what federal agency do the letters FTC stand? _____

2. If the product-content label on a piece of clothing is missing, has a federal law probably been violated?

   _____

3. Why were laws passed requiring sellers to reveal what materials were used in the manufacture of

   clothing products? _____

   _____

4. Examine two pieces of clothing, such as a coat and a sweater, and provide the following:

Kind of Item	Is There a Label?	What Information is on the Label?

7-E. Put a check mark in the columns at the right to indicate whether the following statements are true or false under bankruptcy law.

	True	False
1. Businesses but not individuals may file for bankruptcy.	___	___
2. A record of unpaid debts stays on file for ten years.	___	___
3. If selling all the firm's assets doesn't result in enough cash to pay all its debts, the law excuses the business from paying the remaining debts.	___	___
4. All businesses that file for bankruptcy are declared permanently bankrupt.	___	___
5. Once a firm has been declared bankrupt, it will need to conduct all business forever thereafter for cash.	___	___
6. Any firm may file for bankruptcy again after five years.	___	___
7. A bankrupt firm that starts over again may apply for credit when buying goods.	___	___
8. Business owners declared bankrupt must serve three years or more in prison.	___	___

7-F. Collect examples of two different trademarks from package labels or advertisements. Paste them in the space below and indicate the company that owns the trademark.

Space for Trademark	Company Owning the Trademark

7-G. Place a check mark in the column at the right to indicate whether the item described would be eligible for a patent, copyright, or trademark.

	Patent	Copyright	Trademark
1. Created a computer program to help landscape lawns......................	_____	_____	_____
2. Wrote a ninety-page children's story for day-care center use.	_____	_____	_____
3. Designed a bird-calling device to attract most types of songbirds. ...	_____	_____	_____
4. Created a specially designed pen that would allow a person without hands to write with a foot.	_____	_____	_____
5. Created a new type of flower that always blooms.	_____	_____	_____
6. Developed a new logo for a new firm..	_____	_____	_____

7-H. Many businesses are required to secure a license from a local government (such as a city) before they can operate. Find out if a special license is required for as many of the businesses listed below as are found in your community. Make your report from the following form:

Type of Business	License Required	License Not Required
1. Automobile repair business	_____	_____
2. Bakery	_____	_____
3. Beauty salon or barber shop	_____	_____
4. Bowling alley	_____	_____
5. Dry cleaning business	_____	_____
6. Service station	_____	_____
7. Motel	_____	_____
8. Drug store	_____	_____
9. Restaurant	_____	_____
10. Grocery store	_____	_____

7-I. For the items listed below, indicate if each is primarily a progressive, regressive, or proportional tax.

1. Tax on gasoline for automobiles. _____

2. State income tax rate that rises with every additional $1,000 of annual income earned. _____

3. State sales tax on all items except food, clothing, and home rental fees. _____

4. Real estate taxes on assessed value of home. _____

7-J. Assume the average business tax rates for three countries are as shown below. Also shown is the taxable income for three firms. After studying the information, calculate the tax each business would pay in each country.

		Tax Rate for Countries		
Business Taxable Income		Thailand (40%)	Nicaragua (54%)	Somalia (66%)
A	$ 50,000	_____	_____	_____
B	$ 275,000	_____	_____	_____
C	$2,400,000	_____	_____	_____

7-K. Study the year's information below regarding two individuals who live in a state that has a 6 percent sales tax. Then answer the questions that follow.

		Jennings	Sherrer
a.	Take-home pay	$20,000	$35,000
b.	Amount spent	20,000	26,000
c.	Amount saved	0	9,000
d.	Tax calculation	_____	_____
e.	Amount of tax	_____	_____
f.	Tax rate calculation	_____	_____
g.	Effective tax rate	_____	_____

1. Complete the information needed for lines d through g.

2. Did Jennings or Sherrer benefit most from the tax system? _____

3. Is this a progressive, regressive, or proportional tax? _____

SMALL GROUP ACTIVITIES

Group Activity 1

After reading the following business case, personally decide whether the corporation is right or whether its competitors are right.

A large trucking company, named KOT (Keep On Trucking), has been buying up small trucking firms over the last several years. KOT now does about 75 percent of all interstate trucking but only 40 percent of intrastate trucking. Because of its efficient means of operating a large fleet of trucks nationwide, smaller firms are complaining, saying that a monopoly exists. The Small Truckers Association (STA), however, plans to initiate a lawsuit shortly and will invite other smaller, nationwide trucking firms to join it.

KOT has a large law firm representing it and feels quite certain that it can win such a lawsuit on the grounds that its goal is to offer businesses timely and efficient services that meet their heavy trucking demands on schedule. Small firms are often much slower. Also, the drivers of the small firms do not receive as much training and have a higher accident record. Further, KOT is doing nothing to block the small firms from competing more aggressively. KOT is not interfering with any of their rights or efforts to get larger. This morning STA served formal notice to KOT that it was filing a lawsuit against it.

Team Tasks:

1. Your instructor will form a legal team for KOT and another for STA. Each team of attorneys will have a staff of legal aides assisting it. Half of the remaining students will be assigned to the KOT team and the other half to the STA team. These teams will obtain whatever information the attorney groups need in order to help establish the legal grounds for their attorneys.

2. The KOT team will meet, organize the evidence that can be presented in its case, and delegate requests for information to its staff of legal aides. The STA team will organize to make a plan for winning the case and will request of its legal aides the ammunition to win.

3. The two legal aide groups should immediately dig up all the information possible that would allow their legal teams to win. Use any source available, such as reviews of the AT&T breakup of the country's long distance company some years ago and the more recent case against Microsoft. Read from library and Internet sources as much as possible about how judges decide such cases. For example, are there any guidelines that judges use for deciding when a company is a monopoly? (Many articles appear in business and other journals available in the library or on the Internet.)

4. When the evidence has been gathered and presented to the attorneys, the attorneys for each side will present their views to the judge, who may be your teacher or other designated person. The judge will make a decision, but the losing group may appeal to a federal court or accept the judge's verdict.

Group Activity 2

Many firms declare bankruptcy each year, but not all go out of business. After being assigned a partner by your teacher, your two-person team will need to find answers to these questions:

1. What are the basic procedures to be followed for most types of bankruptcy?
2. Explain why some businesses that have filed for bankruptcy may continue to operate for many years.
3. Identify five or more companies that operate in or near your state that have filed for bankruptcy.
4. Do any bankrupt firms ever recover and become successful?

To research your answers, use the library, the Internet, or a lawyer who handles bankruptcy cases. Prepare a written report for your teacher. Then you and your partner can present an oral report of your findings to your class.

Chapter 8		Scoring Record				
Technology and Information Management	Name _____ Date _____		**Part A**	**Part B**	**Part C**	**Total**
		Perfect score	20	10	5	35
		My score				

Study Guide

Part A—*Directions:* Indicate your answer to each of the following questions by writing either yes or no in the Answers column.

Answers

1. Does the term "information" refer to the original unprocessed facts and figures that businesses have generated? .... 1. _____
2. Does application software manage the computer's file system? .... 2. _____
3. Can the Internet be used as a substitute for phoning? .... 3. _____
4. Do all Web addresses begin with "www."? .... 4. _____
5. Is it possible to access the Internet without an ISP? .... 5. _____
6. Does a search engine allow users to navigate and view Web pages? .... 6. _____
7. Does a LAN usually cover a geographic area, such as a state? .... 7. _____
8. Can e-mail be sent to the Internet through an intranet? .... 8. _____
9. Can an extranet allow a supplier to track a company's inventory records without gaining access to other company data? .... 9. _____
10. Do organizations violate business ethics when they sell information about people who use the Internet to browse or buy merchandise? .... 10. _____
11. Does the Federal Trade Commission require that businesses notify buyers of their rights on how personal information will be used? .... 11. _____
12. Are fingerprints and retina scanning examples of methods being tested to safeguard organizational information? .... 12. _____
13. Is a computer system that processes data into meaningful information called an information system? .... 13. _____
14. Is a system that helps managers consider alternatives in making decisions called a decision support system? .... 14. _____
15. Can an EIS system be used to collect information about competitors or about government policies? .... 15. _____
16. Is it true that managers cannot reduce or eliminate common complaints, such as eye strain and backaches, by workers who use computers for long periods? .... 16. _____
17. Are improper keyboard or chair heights likely to cause hand problems for computer operators? .... 17. _____
18. Has the title for most secretaries changed to one like "administrative assistant" because their roles have changed? .... 18. _____
19. Is it true that help desk employees need technical skills but not "people skills"? .... 19. _____
20. Has the use of computers in business cut paperwork in addition to increasing worker productivity? .... 20. _____

Total Score _____

Part B—*Directions:* For each of the following statements, select the word, or group of words, that best completes the statement. In the Answers column, write the letter corresponding to the answer selected.

1. The typical office computer that most workers use is a (a) laptop, (b) notebook, (c) mainframe, (d) personal computer. .... 1. _____

2. Spreadsheets are used primarily to create (a) written documents, (b) financial statements, (c) graphics, (d) business forms. .... 2. _____

3. Which of the following can be shared on the Web? (a) printed text only, (b) text and videos only, (c) text and photographs only, (d) text, videos, and photographs. .... 3. _____

4. A program that allows users to navigate and view Web pages is called a (a) Netservice program, (b) browser, (c) search engine, (d) telecommunications program. .... 4. _____

5. Who created the World Wide Web? (a) Gordon Moore, (b) Tim Berners-Lee, (c) Intel, (d) Bill Gates. .... 5. _____

6. Which statement is FALSE about CIOs? (a) CIOs do not need management skills. (b) CIOs protect information from being improperly used or getting to people who should not have it. (c) CIOs must know what types of equipment to purchase to meet an organization's needs. (d) CIOs make it possible for all people in the organization who need information to get it easily and quickly. .... 6. _____

7. A computer that stores data and application software for all PC workstations in a single building or building complex is called a (a) search engine, (b) server, (c) browser, (d) bus. .... 7. _____

8. All of the following are types of information systems EXCEPT (a) an MIS, (b) a DSS, (c) an ISP, (d) an EIS. .... 8. _____

9. The ability to consider alternatives by analyzing "what if" scenarios is a key capability of (a) an MIS, (b) a DSS, (c) an EIS, (d) an ISP. .... 9. _____

10. Which statement is NOT true about downsizing? (a) Many firms help employees get retrained. (b) Some firms help employees find new jobs with other firms. (c) Employees may become less productive. (d) Morale improves quickly. .... 10. _____

Total Score _____

Part C—*Directions:* In the Answers column, write the letter of the word or expression in Column I that most closely matches each statement in Column II.

Column I	Column II	Answers
A. Help desk	1. Assists workers with computer problems	_____
B. Network administrator	2. Creates and modifies software programs	_____
C. Programmer	3. Helps create and maintain an MIS	_____
D. Systems analyst	4. Manages and maintains a Web site	_____
E. Telecommuter	5. Uses electronic equipment to work at home	_____
F. Web page designer		
G. Webmaster	Total Score	_____

Directions: Study each controversial issue carefully. Follow the advice of your teacher before listing in the columns provided reasons why people might answer Yes or No. Your teacher may want you to work with a classmate, talk with others in your community to gather information, or use the library or Internet to gather facts.

8-1. Would more people use the Internet to buy goods and services if the privacy of their personal information were better protected than it is today?

Reasons for "Yes"	Reasons for "No"

8-2. Has the extensive and increasing use of electronic technology, such as computers, cell phones, Web sites, and e-mail, reduced the interpersonal relationships in our society to an undesirable level?

Reasons for "Yes"	Reasons for "No"

PROBLEMS

8-A. Check whether the items listed below are more often associated with a traditional office or an electronic office.

Item	Traditional Office	Electronic Office
1. Filing cabinets	___	___
2. Compact disc	___	___
3. Facsimile machine	___	___
4. Typewriter	___	___
5. Cellular phone	___	___
6. Stenographer	___	___
7. Floppy disk	___	___
8. Laser printer	___	___

8-B. Listed below are components of a computer system. Indicate what type of device each component is by placing a check mark in the appropriate column.

Item	Input Devices	Central Processing Unit	Output Devices
a. Computer memory	___	___	___
b. Mouse	___	___	___
c. Monitor	___	___	___
d. Digital camera	___	___	___
e. Hard drive	___	___	___
f. Digital video disk	___	___	___
g. Keyboard	___	___	___
h. Operating system software	___	___	___
i. Scanner	___	___	___
j. Printer	___	___	___

8-C. After each task described, write the name of the type of computer software needed to perform each task.

1. Key a letter or other business document. _____

2. Create a newsletter for the business. _____

3. Prepare accounting financial statements. _____

4. Develop a bar or pie chart. _____

5. Store a variety of information about all employees in a business. _____

8-D. Assume that on an average day, 60 percent of people with Internet access go online. According to the Pew Research Center, surveys indicate the percentage of people online who did each of the following activities "yesterday." Study the information and answer the questions that appear below the table.

Activity	Percent	Activity	Percent
a. Send/read e-mail	52	j. Look for political or campaign news/info.	10
b. Get news (general)	22	k. Look for information about movies, books, or other leisure activities	8
c. Surf the Web for fun	21	l. Get travel information	7
d. Look for information about a hobby or interest	18	m. Get health and medical information	7
e. Check the weather	16	n. Visit a government Web site	7
f. Do work/research online for a job	16	o. Play a game	6
g. Get financial information	15	p. Chat in a chat room	5
h. Look for information on a product/service they are thinking of buying	14	q. Listen to or download music	5
		r. Look for information about a job	5
i. Exchange instant messages	12	s. Purchase products/bid at auction site	4

1. If 121 million Americans used the Internet today, how many of them likely read and/or sent e-mail?

   _____

2. If 201 million Americans have Internet access, how many Americans likely searched for a new job online

   today? _____

3. Assume that 201 million Americans have Internet access. How many each day look for information online

   about a product they are interested in buying, but do not actually make their purchase online?

   _____

   _____

4. What three items on the list most surprise you about how people use the Internet? _____

   _____

   _____

5. Assuming you have Internet access, for which of the five ways listed above do/would you most use the

   Internet? _____

   _____

   _____

   _____

8-E. Michael Armstrong, former CEO of AT&T, reportedly made the following statement: "It took radio 30 years to reach its first 50 million Americans; it took TV 13 years. After only six years, the World Wide Web had 100 million users. With the next advance—broadband technology, which can transfer every issue of *The New York Times* from the last 100 years in just one second—the Web could reach millions even faster." Answer the following questions:

1. How does Moore's Law relate to Mr. Armstrong's statement? _____

   _____

   _____

   _____

2. If Mr. Armstrong made his statement on June 15 of the year 2000, about when did technological advances

   allow *The New York Times* to be transferred in half a second? _____

   _____

   _____

3. Given the time for radio, TV, and the Web to reach large audiences, what general conclusion can you make

   about the speed of technological change? _____

   _____

   _____

8-F. For each item listed, indicate whether it is part of telecommunications by placing a check mark in the appropriate column.

Item	Yes	No
1. An airmail letter sent to Argentina.	____	____
2. A message sent via computer from one floor in a building to another computer located on another floor in the same building.	____	____
3. A chart sent by facsimile from Chicago to Houston.	____	____
4. A contract sent from a manager's computer in Atlanta to a manager's computer in London, England.	____	____
5. A telephone message to a manager in another city left with the receptionist because the line was busy.	____	____

Name _____

8-G. Study the cost of installing a new computer system from the information provided. Then answer the questions below.

	Cost	Percent
1 Server computer	$15,000	_____
10 Desktop computers	12,000	_____
5 Laser printers	4,600	_____
8 Software programs	3,200	_____
Installation	3,800	_____
Training employees	5,200	_____
Total	_____	_____

1. In the Cost column, insert the total cost of the computer system in the answer blank provided.

2. In the Percent column, insert the percentage cost of each component of the system to one decimal place.

3. To what activity should most of the training time be devoted? _____

4. What is the total cost of the various pieces of hardware? _____

5. What percent of the total cost is for hardware and what percent is for other costs?

   a. Hardware: _____

   b. Other Costs: _____

8-H. For each item listed below, indicate by a check mark the appropriate computer network that would handle the task shown.

Item	Intranet	Extranet	Internet
1. Send a memo to another worker located in another building.	_____	_____	_____
2. Send a request to a supplier to ship goods today.	_____	_____	_____
3. An employee checks his health care benefits.	_____	_____	_____
4. A manager searches for a competitor's similar product.................	_____	_____	_____
5. At lunch a worker sends a note to his daughter at home.	_____	_____	_____
6. A firm processes weekly paychecks for a corporation that are sent by computer to the corporation each Friday.	_____	_____	_____

8-I. Check the appropriate column to indicate which computer information system would provide the needed information for each item listed below.

Item	Management Information System	Decision Support System	Executive Information System
1. Find out the total daily sales from each of the eight point-of-sale terminals.	___	___	___
2. Compare yearly total sales to major competitors.	___	___	___
3. Get a breakdown of manufacturing costs for every quarter of the year and consider how to lower them.	___	___	___
4. Obtain total hours worked for each assembly line worker for the last three weeks.	___	___	___
5. Forecast sales for the next three years.	___	___	___
6. Calculate the total cost of goods sold and operating expenses for each month during the past year.	___	___	___
7. Set new product prices based upon the Consumer Price Index.	___	___	___

8-J. Assume that within the next six months, a firm's chief information officer has announced to her managers that voice recognition software for all office workers will be installed that will enable them to dictate words and numbers into their computers with 99 percent accuracy. The managers will face certain problems from employees when they learn of this announcement. As the CIO or a manager, how would you answer the following two questions?

1. What problems will arise and how will you handle them if the task of keying data into computers using keyboards will no longer be necessary and will result in some workers no longer being needed?

_____

_____

_____

_____

_____

_____

_____

2. How will you reorganize or redesign the many jobs that involve some keying of data?

_____

_____

_____

_____

_____

_____

_____

SMALL GROUP ACTIVITIES

Group Activity 1

Background

A common term today is "sick building." It means that the building or objects in the building are causing employees to become ill. Those objects can be chairs, desks, carpets, or tobacco smoke. In addition, computers, keyboards, lighting, and the adjustability of chair height and backs may contribute to health problems. The construction material in buildings may also affect one's health. Factory equipment may injure some workers.

Employee lawsuits caused by dangerous equipment, dangerous vapors, and unclean air circulating throughout buildings are increasing. Poor circulation is a primary contributor, because air with dangerous elements in it is often not adequately replaced by fresh air fast enough. The sad fact is that old as well as new buildings may be sick. Evidence suggests that fixing sick buildings reduces accidents and illnesses. Employee absences decrease, and productivity climbs.

Instructions

Your instructor will put you into small groups for the purpose of gathering information and conducting interviews about sick buildings in the work climate. Here are your tasks:

1. Each team member should obtain and report to fellow team members the key points made in a magazine article dealing with sick buildings. One example would be "Is Your Office Killing You?" by Michelle Conlin in *Business Week,* June 5, 2000.

2. Once your team has reviewed and shared information from the magazine articles, identify a profit or not-for-profit organization with 10 or more employees. With the approval of the managers and your teacher, interview managers and workers at the organization. Or, interview people at shopping malls or in different neighborhoods about their workplaces.

3. Obtain answers to the following questions, and add other questions with your teacher's approval:
   a. Has your health or the health of other workers ever been affected by the building in which you work?
   b. What health problems have you or other employees experienced?
   c. What building conditions exist, or might exist, that you believe would cause or contribute to your health problems?
   d. Has your doctor indicated the possible cause or causes of your condition that might be related to the building in which you work?
   e. Have you informed your employer about the effect of the building on your health or that of other employees?
   f. Has any action been taken to improve the condition of the building, such as replacing or improving ventilation?

Final Action

Your team should summarize the information gathered from magazines and the surveys and then present an oral report to the class. If requested by your teacher, prepare a written group report. Include tables and diagrams in both your oral and written reports.

Group Activity 2

Your teacher will place you into groups of three to five students. Your group is to find out from other students in your school or community what types and brands of software and hardware they own or use away from school. With your group, prepare a questionnaire. Select one of the following topics: operating system software, application software, input devices, output devices, or computer systems (Dell, Compaq, Apple, etc.). Once your group has selected its topic, obtain approval from your instructor.

Each questionnaire can be quite simple and should contain between five and ten questions. The questions can be of different types, such as yes/no, checklists, and fill-in-the-blanks. Each student should first individually create five questions for his or her group. The group should then meet to review the questions and to reduce and refine the list to not more than ten clear questions. Now test your questionnaire on about five students in order to improve the wording of the questions. Revise the questionnaire as needed. You can administer the questionnaire orally and record student responses on your copy.

After collecting the answers, meet as a group and sort out the answers, prepare tables of answers, and calculate percentages. Use a graphics or presentation software, such as PowerPoint, to prepare tables and charts to show on a screen. Make an oral report to the class of your questionnaire answers. Draw conclusions about the popularity of what students use most and least.

		Scoring Record			
	Name _____		Part A	Part B	Part C	Total
		Perfect score	20	15	5	40
	Date _____	My score				

Study Guide

Part A—*Directions:* Indicate your answer to each of the following questions by writing either yes or no in the Answers column.

Answers

1. Does the United States lead the world in Internet users with over 50% of all users?......... 1. _____
2. Has the Internet allowed many small businesses to compete successfully with larger, established companies? .... 2. _____
3. According to the U.S. Department of Commerce, does the total amount of U.S. Internet sales to consumers exceed $130 billion?.. 3. _____
4. Does the dollar volume of consumer Internet sales exceed the dollar value of business-to-business sales?.. 4. _____
5. Is internal and external communication the main use of the Internet by businesses?......... 5. _____
6. Is an advantage of using e-mail the increased speed of communications? .... 6. _____
7. Is much of the information on the Internet provided free by government agencies, colleges and universities, libraries, and private businesses?.. 7. _____
8. Is it possible for businesses to benefit from promotion on the Internet without actually selling products online? .... 8. _____
9. Must a company be either a bricks-and-mortar company or a dot-com company?............. 9. _____
10. Does the interaction stage of e-commerce development allow customers to complete an entire sales transaction online?.. 10. _____
11. Are the most frequently Internet-purchased consumer items books, office supplies, computer hardware, and electronics? .... 11. _____
12. Has the Internet Advertising Bureau established standards for the size and appearance of Internet advertisements?.. 12. _____
13. Do most consumers still purchase most of their products from bricks-and-mortar businesses, even if they use the Internet to gather product information? .... 13. _____
14. Are online shoppers proving to be less brand and store loyal?.. 14. _____
15. Is the Webby award given to organizations with the most effective Web site designs? ..... 15. _____
16. Is security one of the main concerns of online shoppers?.. 16. _____
17. Is the first step in establishing an e-commerce Web site to determine the purpose of the Web site?.. 17. _____
18. Is it important to know the age of your customers before designing your Web site?......... 18. _____
19. Must all domain names be registered?.. 19. _____
20. Should you include your domain name on all company materials?.. 20. _____

Total Score _____

Part B—*Directions:* For each of the following statements, select the word, or group of words, that best completes the statement. In the Answers column, write the letter corresponding to the answer selected.

1. The Internet has allowed many small businesses to (a) compete with larger, established businesses, (b) reach customers all over the world, (c) exchange business-related information, (d) do all of these. ....

    1. _____

2. Approximately what percent of all sales by businesses to consumers is completed using the Internet? (a) 1%, (b) 2.5%, (c) 50%, (d) 80%. ....

    2. _____

3. The Internet was first devised as (a) a method of sending personal e-mail messages, (b) a military and research tool, (c) a way to advertise products and services electronically, (d) all of these responses. ....

    3. _____

4. It is reported that in 2004, business-to-business sales on the Internet totaled approximately (a) $8 billion, (b) $45 billion, (c) $200 billion, (d) $1.95 trillion. ....

    4. _____

5. The Internet is used for (a) personal communications, (b) business-to-business communications, (c) business-to-customer communications, (d) all of these. ....

    5. _____

6. Salespeople who log onto a company Web site and check inventory levels are demonstrating what use of the Internet? (a) business communications, (b) information gathering, (c) business operations, (d) all of these uses. ....

    6. _____

7. When a customer completes a registration card, what use of the Internet is being demonstrated? (a) business communications, (b) information gathering, (c) business operations, (d) all of these uses. ....

    7. _____

8. A dot-com business (a) usually has a bricks-and-mortar headquarters, (b) is a company that does almost all of its business activities through the Internet, (c) is typically an outgrowth of a bricks-and-mortar business, (d) is always a small business. ....

    8. _____

9. If a business has a Web site where customers can search a product database, download a catalog, and print an order form to be mailed or faxed to the company, the Web site is (a) interactive, (b) integrated, (c) informational, (d) all of these. ....

    9. _____

10. A business Web site that allows consumers only to learn about the company and its products is (a) interactive, (b) fully integrated, (c) informational, (d) transactional. ....

    10. _____

11. Today, most consumers go online to (a) purchase products, (b) gather information, (c) view product advertisements, (d) communicate. ....

    11. _____

12. Which factor is the most important to consumers when shopping online? (a) a company telephone number, (b) lower prices than at bricks-and-mortar businesses, (c) an easy-to-use Web site with effective customer service, (d) online coupons. ....

    12. _____

13. When establishing an e-commerce Web site, which of the following steps should be the final one before opening the business? (a) determine the purpose of your Web site, (b) advertise the online business, (c) study your customers, their needs, and their Internet experiences, (d) obtain a Web server and a domain name. ....

    13. _____

14. A pixel is (a) an advertisement on the Web, (b) one or more dots that act as the smallest unit on a video display screen, (c) another name for an e-commerce business, (d) a Web-hosting service.

    14. _____

15. Programs that keep track of online shoppers' selections and allow them to submit their orders for processing are called (a) electronic shopping carts, (b) integrated order forms, (c) interactive protocols, (d) hyperlinks. ....

    15. _____

Total Score _____

Part C—*Directions:* In the Answers column, write the letter of the word or expression in Column I that most closely matches each statement in Column II.

Column I	Column II	Answers
A. e-commerce	1. The address for locating an online business	_____
B. pixel	2. Doing business online	
C. dot-com	3. Stage of Web site development that allows customers to complete a product purchase online	_____
D. bricks-and-mortar		
E. integration	4. Unit of measure used for determining the size of Internet advertisements	_____
F. interaction		
G. domain name	5. Businesses that sell most of their products online	_____
	Total Score	_____

Name _____

Directions: Study each controversial issue carefully. Follow the advice of your teacher before listing in the columns provided reasons why people might answer Yes or No. Your teacher may want you to work with a class-mate, talk with others in your community to gather information, or use the library or Internet to gather facts.

9-1. Should businesses that gather information online by asking customers to fill out warranty or registration cards sell that information to other businesses without the customers' permission?

Reasons for "Yes"	Reasons for "No"

9-2. Should people be prevented from registering the established name of a business, product, or celebrity with which they have no direct association?

Reasons for "Yes"	Reasons for "No"

PROBLEMS

9-A. In the year 2006, the number of regular Internet users worldwide was estimated at 1 billion people. Using the following information showing the percentage of users by country taken from Figure 9-2 of the textbook, calculate the number of Internet users in each country. Then determine the number and percentage of users in all other countries.

Country	% of Users	Number of Users
United States	20.1%	_____
China	10.9%	_____
Japan	8.4%	_____
India	5.0%	_____
Germany	4.8%	_____
United Kingdom	3.7%	_____
Korea (South)	3.3%	_____
All other countries	_____	_____

9-B. Both bricks-and-mortar and dot-com businesses maintain Web sites. However, by visiting a Web site, you should be able to identify which businesses have one or more physical locations where they sell products and which use e-commerce as the primary method of selling products. Using the Internet or business information and advertising in magazines, newspapers, or telephone directories, identify five bricks-and-mortar businesses and five dot-com businesses. In the column on the right, list the primary information you found that identified the appropriate classification for the business.

CATEGORY OF BUSINESS	REASON FOR CLASSIFICATION

Bricks-and-Mortar

1. _____   _____

2. _____   _____

3. _____   _____

4. _____   _____

5. _____   _____

Dot-Com

1. _____   _____

2. _____   _____

3. _____   _____

4. _____   _____

5. _____   _____

Name _____

9-C. Businesses use the Internet for a number of purposes in addition to selling products and services to customers. Select a business that you might like to own and operate. Then answer the following questions to identify the ways you could use the Internet in that business.

The type of business I might like to own and operate is _____

1. If you were going to use the Internet for communications in your business:
    With whom would you communicate?   For what purpose?

    _____   _____
    _____   _____
    _____   _____

2. If you were going to use the Internet for information gathering in your business:
    What information would you need?   What information source would you use?

    _____   _____
    _____   _____
    _____   _____

3. If you were going to use the Internet to improve the business operations of your business:
    What operations would you improve?   How would the Internet benefit your business?

    _____   _____
    _____   _____
    _____   _____

9-D. Businesses using e-commerce will be in one of three stages of development—information stage, interaction stage, or integration stage. Search the Internet to identify three businesses in each of the stages. In the following chart, list the company name, the Internet address, and the evidence from the Web site you used to identify the developmental stage.

INFORMATION STAGE

Company Name	Internet Address	Evidence

INTERACTION STAGE

Company Name	Internet Address	Evidence

INTEGRATION STAGE

Company Name	Internet Address	Evidence

9-E. The following boxes illustrate common sizes of Internet advertisements. Use an Internet browser to locate an example of a business advertisement for each of the sizes shown that you believe is particularly effective in promoting the business or product. Re-create each advertisement by drawing it in the appropriate space. For each size, write a short statement that identifies why you believe the ad design is effective.

Full Banner

Half Banner

Vertical Banner

Button

Micro Button

The reason I believe the advertisement is effective:

Full Banner: _____

_____

_____

Half Banner: _____

_____

_____

Vertical Banner: _____

_____

_____

_____

Button: _____

_____

_____

Micro Button: _____

_____

_____

9-F. The Internet allows businesses to direct their products and services toward very specific groups of customers. Search the Internet and identify two businesses that appear to be marketing their products and services to each of the identified groups. For each, list the products and services the business is selling on the Web.

Customer Group	Business	Products and Services Offered
New Parents	_____	_____
	_____	_____
Teenagers	_____	_____
	_____	_____
Musicians	_____	_____
	_____	_____
Other Businesses	_____	_____
	_____	_____
Travelers	_____	_____
	_____	_____

Now identify three other customer groups for which you have located e-commerce businesses that are marketing their products and services to the specific group.

_____	_____	_____
	_____	_____
_____	_____	_____
	_____	_____
_____	_____	_____
	_____	_____

9-G. The following steps allow you to make the initial decisions necessary to develop an online business. Answer each of the following questions to complete each step.

1. What is the purpose of your Web site? _____

    _____

    _____

2. Who will be the primary customers you want to visit your Web site? _____

    _____

    _____

3. What products and services will you offer? Will your site be informational, interactive, or integrated?

    _____

    _____

    _____

4. What domain name would you like to use for your Web site? (Check with an online registration service to

    see if it is available.) What Web-hosting service will you use? (Search the Internet to find a service.)

    _____

    _____

    _____

5. What electronic shopping cart software would you use? (Search the Internet to identify available software,

    features, and costs.) _____

    _____

    _____

6. What will your business's home page look like? (Develop a design using a computer-based drawing pro-

    gram or by hand-drawing.) _____

    _____

    _____

7. What are two primary locations where you will advertise your business? Design one Internet advertise-

    ment that introduces your business. _____

    _____

    _____

SMALL GROUP ACTIVITIES

Group Activity 1

A number of organizations recognize the top Internet Web sites with awards, such as the Webby awards presented by the International Academy of Digital Arts and Sciences. Form a team with three or four other classmates to complete the following activities.

1. Search the Internet to identify the best home page for an e-commerce business. When your team has agreed on the best site, print a copy of the home page using a color printer.
2. Following your teacher's instructions, cooperate with the other teams to develop an exhibit of posters displaying all teams' printed home pages. Clearly identify each home page with the company name.
3. Display the exhibit in a central location in the school with a ballot box, copies of ballots that list each of the companies, and a blank space by each name on the ballot for voting.
4. Ask teachers and students in your school to vote for the home page they believe is the best business Web site design. When the voting is finished, tally the ballots and post the results so everyone knows which business received the most votes.

Group Activity 2

Following your teacher's instructions, form teams to complete the following activity. With your teammates, identify a business in your community that uses e-commerce. The business can be a dot-com business or a bricks-and-mortar business. Arrange an interview with the owner or manager of the business, and ask the following questions:

1. Why did you decide to use e-commerce in your business?

   _____

   _____

   _____

   _____

2. What steps did you follow to establish e-commerce in your business?

   _____

   _____

   _____

   _____

3. What were the most important resources you used to learn about e-commerce and to develop the e-commerce business?

   _____

   _____

   _____

   _____

4. What percentage of your business comes from e-commerce? Is the percentage increasing, decreasing, or staying about the same? Are the customers who use e-commerce different from those who do not?

_____

_____

_____

_____

5. What are the most positive and the most negative aspects of operating an e-commerce business? What improvements, if any, do you plan to make in your e-commerce business?

_____

_____

_____

_____

When your team has completed the interview, prepare a written report of what you learned to share and discuss with the other teams. When all teams have completed their reports, join in a class discussion to determine what was similar and different among the e-commerce businesses.

Study Guide

Part A—*Directions:* Indicate your answer to each of the following questions by writing either yes or no in the Answers column.

Answers

1. Is "communication" defined as "the sending of information"? .... 1. _____
2. Does the receiver of communication have a responsibility to try to understand the message as the sender intended? .... 2. _____
3. Is a distraction created when two students whisper during a class presentation? .... 3. _____
4. Are messages usually distorted unconsciously? .... 4. _____
5. Is avoiding eye contact considered a form of body language? .... 5. _____
6. Do nonverbal messages convey as much meaning as do verbal messages? .... 6. _____
7. Is it possible for outsiders to access a company's e-mail messages? .... 7. _____
8. Might abusive sexual language in e-mail messages lead to a lawsuit by offended employees? 8. _____
9. Is information overload a rare complaint of employees? .... 9. _____
10. Is spam unsolicited advertising that finds its way into e-mail boxes? .... 10. _____
11. Do many emoticons make a message seem professional? .... 11. _____
12. Are distrust and secrecy apt to be found in open cultures? .... 12. _____
13. Do employees often fear revealing negative information and avoid making honest criticisms in closed cultures? .... 13. _____
14. Should managers usually try to block informal communication channels in a business? .... 14. _____
15. Are grapevine messages usually accurate? .... 15. _____
16. Is time lost attending meetings considered a major disadvantage of meetings? .... 16. _____
17. Are wild and imaginative ideas encouraged during brainstorming sessions? .... 17. _____
18. Does a win/lose strategy to resolve a conflict occur when everyone involved in the conflict agrees to a mutually acceptable solution? .... 18. _____
19. Does how close a person stands when talking to someone else differ from one country to another? .... 19. _____
20. Is the written communication channel best when managers want to communicate information about a new policy? .... 20. _____

Total Score _____

Part B—*Directions:* For each of the following statements, select the word, or group of words, that best completes the statement. In the Answers column, write the letter corresponding to the answer selected.

Answers

1. Which is NOT a form of communication feedback? (a) returning a questionnaire, (b) restating the sender's message in your own words, (c) asking questions to clarify a point, (d) assuming a message is understood. .... 1. _____

2. Which statement is true about distortions? (a) Self-enhancement is not a form of distortion. (b) Self-protection is not a form of distortion. (c) Giving an employee a deserved poor rating is not a form of distortion. (d) An exaggeration about one's personal performance is not a form of distortion. .... 2. _____

3. Carelessly prepared messages reflect (a) neutrally on the writer only, (b) neutrally on the organization only, (c) negatively on the writer and on the organization, (d) negatively on the writer only. .... 3. _____

4. When creativity and problem solving are encouraged at all levels and trust and confidence exist to a high degree in an organization, what type of communication system exists? (a) open, (b) upward, (c) downward, (d) closed. .... 4. _____

5. How does the nominal group technique (NGT) differ from a regular meeting of workers involved in solving a problem? (a) The NGT requires everyone to agree on the solution. (b) The NGT requires open voting. (c) The NGT requires all members to offer solutions. (d) The NGT forces the manager to select the solution. .... 5. _____

6. Which statement is FALSE about conflicts? (a) Conflicts that are not resolved often result in long-term problems. (b) Conflicts sometimes are an obstacle to job performance. (c) Conflicts do not lead to healthy discussions. (d) Conflicts may occur between groups. .... 6. _____

7. When conflicts are relatively unimportant, which strategy should managers use? (a) avoidance, (b) compromise, (c) win/lose, (d) interference. .... 7. _____

8. What has the typical international business done to help prepare managers who are about to be transferred to foreign countries? (a) Educate the manager on how to teach the workers in the new country to speak English. (b) Encourage the manager to make social contacts with English-speaking people in the new country. (c) Provide intensive training in the culture and language of the new country. (d) Provide a dictionary for the language of the new country. .... 8. _____

9. Which of the ten rules of good listening is the one on which all others depend? (a) Ask questions. (b) Hold your temper. (c) Be patient. (d) Stop talking! .... 9. _____

10. The best way to deliver a compliment to an employee for excellent work is (a) orally to personalize it, (b) in writing in order to record it, (c) both orally and in writing, (d) orally in a private meeting. .... 10. _____

Total Score _____

Part C—*Directions:* In the Answers column, write the letter of the word or expression in Column I that most closely matches each statement in Column II.

Column I	Column II	Answers
A. brainstorming	1. Sharing ideas, beliefs, and opinions	_____
B. closed culture	2. Someone slams a door	_____
C. communication	3. How people consciously or unconsciously change messages	_____
D. conflict	4. A discussion technique that stimulates ideas	_____
E. culture	5. Develops when interfering with the achievement of another person's goals	_____
F. distortion		
G. distraction		
H. grapevine	Total Score	_____

Chapter 10: Controversial Issues   Name _____

Directions: Study each controversial issue carefully. Follow the advice of your teacher before listing in the columns provided reasons why people might answer Yes or No. Your teacher may want you to work with a classmate, talk with others in your community to gather information, or use the library or Internet to gather facts.

10-1. Do employers have the right to examine all e-mail messages before, during, and after working hours from business computers and to punish workers who use business computers for non-business purposes?

Reasons for "Yes"	Reasons for "No"

10-2. Should most meetings be limited to 30 minutes because so much valuable work time is lost talking about trivial business and non-business matters?

Reasons for "Yes"	Reasons for "No"

PROBLEMS

10-A. Check whether each of the following situations describing a barrier to communication is a distraction or a distortion.

	Distraction	Distortion
1. During a meeting, a worker throws a wad of paper into a wastebasket located across the room.	_____	_____
2. A lawyer's beeper beeps during a conversation with a client.	_____	_____
3. When the receptionist told her manager he had a call, she neglected to say that the call was from the doctor who had just completed major surgery on the manager's wife.	_____	_____
4. A client's name was misspelled on an otherwise well-written message.	_____	_____
5. Telephone calls constantly interrupted the manager, who was composing an important report.	_____	_____
6. A supervisor had a serious problem with an employee. When reporting to the manager, the supervisor merely said, "One of my employees has a small problem, but I'm sure it can be worked out."	_____	_____
7. "Skip the minor details, Cindy. What are the important points?"	_____	_____
8. "At today's meeting, please don't mention that some of the gang was smoking again, because written warnings or pink slips will be issued. Instead, let's ask for a discussion of the importance of not smoking in the plant."	_____	_____

10-B. For each of the following communication situations, identify (a) the sender, (b) the receiver, and (c) the message channel.

1. A customer calls the service manager of an auto-repair shop to make an appointment to have her car repaired.

    a. sender _____

    b. receiver _____

    c. message channel _____

2. A sales manager sends an e-mail message to the head of the accounting department, requesting a report on customers who have not paid their balances owed.

    a. sender _____

    b. receiver _____

    c. message channel _____

3. While they are working, Jack tells Colleen about a rumor that some other employees might get an increase in pay next month.

    a. sender _____

    b. receiver _____

    c. message channel _____

4. The branch manager of the Redlands National Bank sends Harvey Kwolek a computerized form letter to inform him that his checking account is overdrawn.

    a. sender _____

    b. receiver _____

    c. message channel _____

Name _____

10-C. On the line to the right of each listed "feeling" that people might express in e-mail messages, hand print the keyboard strokes that best represent the feeling. If you are not aware of an emoticon to express the feeling, create one.

1. Happiness _____

2. Sadness _____

3. Person is tongue-tied _____

4. Wink _____

5. Just kidding _____

6. Someone wearing a walkman _____

7. Someone wearing glasses _____

8. Create one of your own _____

10-D. By checking the appropriate column, indicate whether the nonverbal message confirms or contradicts the verbal message.

	Verbal Message	Nonverbal Message	Confirms	Contradicts
1.	"Please sit and listen, students."	Snaps fingers.	_____	_____
2.	"I'll wait patiently for another five minutes."	Taps fingers on the desk.	_____	_____
3.	"Sure. I'll be happy to work on that project."	Turns eyes toward window and drops voice.	_____	_____
4.	"I'm thinking . . . I'm thinking."	Looks downward and places finger over lips.	_____	_____
5.	"I'm interested in your ideas."	Leans toward person with steady eye contact.	_____	_____

10-E. Place a check mark in one of the two columns on the right for each item below that describes a characteristic within an organization.

Corporate Culture

		Open	Closed
1.	Employees call their bosses by their first names and eat in the same cafeteria.	_____	_____
2.	Employees may send their complaints using e-mail directly to upper-level managers, who respond quickly.	_____	_____
3.	All contact about business matters must be done through formal appointments, at meetings, or by memos.	_____	_____
4.	Informal communication methods are discouraged, and most messages flow downward.	_____	_____
5.	Self-directed work teams were introduced but failed because most managers would not surrender authority.	_____	_____

10-F. How do you handle conflict situations? Place a "1" in the column that represents your preferred strategy and a "2" in the column that represents your second-choice strategy. Discuss answers with your classmates to compare similarities and differences.

Conflict Situations	Avoid	Strategies Compromise	Win/Lose
1. An office mate who is a good friend wants to take her daily mid-morning break with you at 10:00 a.m., but another friend definitely prefers 10:30.	____	____	____
2. Two other managers cannot agree on what amount should be budgeted for hiring a part-time worker who will help all three of you. They turn to you for support.	____	____	____
3. Two co-workers are moving with you to a new office area. Both want the larger desk that overlooks a courtyard. Although you work well with one co-worker, you do not get along with the other. However, you also want the desk that overlooks the courtyard.	____	____	____
4. Your sales manager promised an added cash award to the person with the highest weekly sales. You and five other salespeople want to win the award.	____	____	____
5. A newly hired worker was just promoted. Because you had worked longer and harder, you complained bitterly to your supervisor and accused him of showing favoritism. You stormed out of the office and now must decide what to do.	____	____	____

10-G. The results of a survey of 675 workers in a recent year produced the following answers to this question: "How would you rate your manager's willingness to listen to new ideas and suggestions for improvement?" The responses appear below, followed by questions to be answered.

Very willing 38%
Somewhat willing 44%
Not willing at all 15%
Don't know or no answer 3%

1. How many workers responded to each choice? (Round answers to the nearest whole number.)

   _____

   _____

   _____

2. How many of the workers believed their managers were willing to listen to their ideas?

   _____

3. Based on the answers to the survey, does it appear that managers generally have open-door policies and

   encourage employees to talk with them? _____

   _____

4. Does the study show that most managers support and practice an open culture?

_____

5. What advice would you give the heads of the firms for which the employees work?

_____

_____

_____

_____

10-H. A new president for a business that has problems just hired you as its communications expert. As your first task, the president wants to know how you would handle the following situations, which have occurred regularly over the past several months. Provide two suggestions for each situation.

1. "Whenever a problem arises, everyone has a solution, but no one does anything because everyone talks and no one listens."

   a. _____

   b. _____

2. "I never know whether to chew someone out on the phone, in person, or by memo. Of course, the same question applies to praising a good worker or informing workers of new policies."

   a. _____

   b. _____

   _____

3. "My managers seem great at communicating down to others, but not enough information flows upward."

   a. _____

   b. _____

4. "Our workers don't talk to their managers enough. They do their jobs, but often there are errors because they don't understand the instructions. Not even the managers talk to one another enough."

   a. _____

   b. _____

10-I. Read each of the communications situations described below. For each situation, indicate whether oral or written communications will be more effective by checking the appropriate column.

Situation	Type of Communication Written	Oral
1. A manager wants to tell a few employees how to use a new cash register.	_____	_____
2. An employee wants to tell the company president about a more efficient way to unload merchandise from trucks.	_____	_____
3. A committee chairperson wants to describe a new assignment to committee members.	_____	_____
4. A sales manager needs to give all salespeople a new set of list prices for products.	_____	_____
5. A worker wants to tell another worker her opinion of the new manager.	_____	_____
6. The president of a corporation wants to summarize the year's activities of the company for the stockholders.	_____	_____
7. A group leader wants the group to determine several ways to solve a problem.	_____	_____
8. A large company wants all employees to know about several recent promotions.	_____	_____

SMALL GROUP ACTIVITIES

Group Activity 1

Background

Good writers and speakers, especially in business, are careful about the words they select when writing memos, e-mail messages, letters, advertisements, and press releases for newspapers. The chairperson of a meeting or a public speaker must be equally careful in selecting words that match the audience's backgrounds. Many words such as "cat" are neutral, but people often assign emotional feelings to neutral words. To one person a cat is one's best friend, and to another, a selfish, independent creature. One emotional reaction is positive while the other is negative.

Good writers must consider their readers thoughtfully before picking key words for employees, customers, and others. Generally, writers should select words that the typical reader will see positively, not negatively. That is why the former Complaint Department in stores is now typically named the Service Department. Similarly, "physically handicapped" people are now referred to as "physically challenged." Do you see the difference? Avoid words that contain an undesirable bias, because you want the reader or listener to feel respected, not degraded.

Directions

Your instructor will place you into groups of three to five people. In the diagram below, each group member is to study the neutral nouns in the first column and then to jot on a small slip of paper what emotions or feelings the word gives to him or her. Two examples are provided. Then each student is to reveal his or her written feelings by a word or phrase. Group members should discuss each term and their collective feelings about it. Determine whether each term is more positive or negative and why it is. Record the feelings of others in the second and third columns as well as your own.

Neutral (Noun)	Positive	Negative
Retiree	Friend	Complainer
Bank	Savings	Rich
Work		
Group Meetings		
Corporation		
Entrepreneur		
Credit		
Economics		
Union		
BMW		

The group should now discuss how this exercise could provide them with insights about how to compose business messages orally or in writing. Be prepared to report those ideas to the class when called upon to do so.

Group Activity 2

Effective managers in firms with open cultures often involve their workers in solving problems. Different techniques such as brainstorming and the nominal group technique (NGT) often prove useful for tough problems. For this group activity, the class will be divided in half to form Team A and Team B. Each team will address one of two serious problems that face those who are in charge of the school's largest and newest computer lab. Your instructor will provide both teams with general instructions. Review the steps in Figure 10-6 in the text for using the NGT. Here are the problems to be solved:

Team A's Problem: The first problem to be solved is to safeguard the school's newest instructional computer lab from thieves. Strangers seem to enter unseen and take computer-related equipment because of lax security. Some teachers believe thefts occur mostly during the breaks between classes and when the lab is left open for students to use to do homework during the school day. This security problem needs to be solved soon.

Team B's Problem: The second problem has gotten worse with each passing week. Hackers have been breaking into the system on a fairly regular basis. Virus scares are frequent, and sometimes the system is down for days, upsetting students and instructors. The lab aide has had to work overtime on a somewhat regular basis. Both problems reduce the effectiveness of instruction and are costing taxpayers money.

Your instructor will provide all team members with any special instructions. Each team is expected to generate many ideas for solving their problem. From the list of possible solutions, the three most effective and practical ones will be presented to the instructor and class. The entire class can then discuss and select the one or two best suggestions for solving each problem.

Chapter 11			Scoring Record			
Management Functions and Decision Making	Name _____ Date _____			Part A	Part B	Part C	Total
		Perfect score	25	10	5	40
		My score				

Study Guide

Part A—*Directions:* Indicate your answer to each of the following questions by writing either yes or no in the Answers column.

Answers

1. Will most people who want to become managers start their management careers as supervisors? .... 1. _____
2. Are managers responsible for the success or failure of a company? .... 2. _____
3. Do all managers perform certain activities no matter what the type or size of the company or in what part of the business they work? .... 3. _____
4. Is the primary work of all managers grouped within the six functions: planning, organizing, controlling, implementing, decision making, and supervising? .... 4. _____
5. Do many employees of a business complete management activities? .... 5. _____
6. Would an experienced employee who is given the responsibility to be the leader of a group project be classified as a manager? .... 6. _____
7. In order to be a manager, does a person have to complete all of the management functions and have authority over other jobs and people? .... 7. _____
8. Do most supervisors spend all of their time on management activities? .... 8. _____
9. Do a manager's responsibilities remain the same after he or she is promoted within the organization? .... 9. _____
10. Are most supervisors promoted into management in the same area in which they have worked? .... 10. _____
11. Are supervisors responsible for implementing the plans of executives by getting employees to perform effectively on a day-to-day basis? .... 11. _____
12. Are employee performance reviews a typical supervisory responsibility? .... 12. _____
13. Do most employees prefer to work for managers who are interested in them and their ideas? 13. _____
14. Can a supervisor contribute to the profitability of the company by controlling costs in the area where he or she works? .... 14. _____
15. Is a work schedule an important tool for supervisors to use in daily planning? .... 15. _____
16. Is much of the communication between supervisors and their employees done orally? ...... 16. _____
17. Should most supervisors spend more time on nonmanagerial activities and less time on management functions? .... 17. _____
18. Does every company, whether it is small or large, need a management information system as an important management tool? .... 18. _____
19. When managers use a management information system, do they spend more time on controlling activities? .... 19. _____
20. Do even small companies usually have research departments? .... 20. _____
21. Do business problems generally have only one solution? .... 21. _____
22. Do the terms "problem" and "symptom" mean essentially the same thing? .... 22. _____
23. Are customers a potential source of possible solutions to business problems? .... 23. _____
24. Are studying and evaluating the results of solutions to problems a part of the planning function for managers? .... 24. _____
25. Once a solution to a problem is implemented in a company, should a manager avoid changing the solution even if evidence suggests it is not working well? .... 25. _____

Total Score _____

Part B—*Directions:* For each of the following statements, select the word, or group of words, that best completes the statement. In the Answers column, write the letter corresponding to the answer selected.

1. Employees will be most successful when they move into a management position if (a) they have worked for a poor supervisor so they know what not to do, (b) they begin work as a supervisor before receiving training, (c) they have the chance to try supervision before making a final decision, (d) they have done all of these. .... 1. _____

2. Which of the following is most likely to perform all of the management functions? (a) a small business owner, (b) the top executive of a multinational corporation, (c) a middle manager, (d) all of these. .... 2. _____

3. The type of manager who works most directly with employees on a daily basis is (a) an executive, (b) a mid-manager, (c) a supervisor, (d) none of these. .... 3. _____

4. Which of the following is NOT one of the common responsibilities of supervisors? (a) communicating goals and directions, (b) motivating employees to work effectively, (c) keeping management informed of employee ideas and concerns, (d) developing long-range plans for the organization. .... 4. _____

5. Which of the following activities of supervisors relates most directly to quality control? (a) developing work schedules, (b) developing and checking standards, (c) using effective listening skills, (d) setting priorities so that the most important work gets done. .... 5. _____

6. The effectiveness of a supervisor's job is determined by which factor? (a) the quality of the work of the supervised employees, (b) the efficient use of the company's resources, (c) the satisfaction of the supervisor's employees, (d) all of these. .... 6. _____

7. To manage time efficiently, supervisors must be able to (a) determine the work to be done, (b) set priorities for the most important work, (c) ensure that the work is completed properly and on time, (d) do all of these activities. .... 7. _____

8. A difficult situation requiring a solution is (a) a problem, (b) a symptom, (c) a standard, (d) an alternative. .... 8. _____

9. Which of the following would NOT be appropriate in selecting the solution to be implemented to solve an important problem? (a) take time rather than make a quick decision, (b) involve others to help with the decision, (c) select the least expensive solution, (d) all of these would not be appropriate. .... 9. _____

10. Analyzing the solutions involves (a) brainstorming ideas, (b) listing advantages and disadvantages, (c) determining symptoms, (d) identifying the problem. .... 10. _____

Total Score _____

Part C—*Directions:* In the Answers column, write the letter of the word or expression in Column I that most closely matches each statement in Column II.

Column I	Column II	Answers
A. planning	1. Accomplishing the goals of an organization through the effective use of people and other resources	_____
B. organizing		
C. implementing	2. Deciding how plans can most effectively be accomplished and arranging resources to complete work	_____
D. controlling		
E. management	3. Evaluating results to determine if the company's objectives have been accomplished as planned	_____
	4. Analyzing information and making decisions about what needs to be done	_____
	5. Carrying out the plans and helping employees to work effectively	_____

Total Score _____

Directions: Study each controversial issue carefully. Follow the advice of your teacher before listing in the columns provided reasons why people might answer Yes or No. Your teacher may want you to work with a classmate, talk with others in your community to gather information, or use the library or Internet to gather facts.

11-1. Since supervisors are responsible for the day-to-day operations of a business, are they more important to the success of the business than executives who are responsible for long-range planning and direction of the business?

Reasons for "Yes"	Reasons for "No"

11-2. Should supervisors be selected from among the employees who are the top performers in their areas rather than being selected from those who have the ability to work well with and motivate other employees?

Reasons for "Yes"	Reasons for "No"

PROBLEMS

11-A. All managers perform four functions: planning, organizing, implementing, and controlling. While each manager completes all functions, managers at different levels in a business spend more time on some functions than on others. One company collected information on the average number of hours spent by executives, mid-managers, and supervisors each week completing each of the functions. The results were:

	Planning	Organizing	Implementing	Controlling
Executives	24	15	12	8
Mid-managers	17	15	9	14
Supervisors	6	10	16	12

Complete the following figure by shading in the appropriate sections representing the percentage of work time spent by each group of managers during the week.

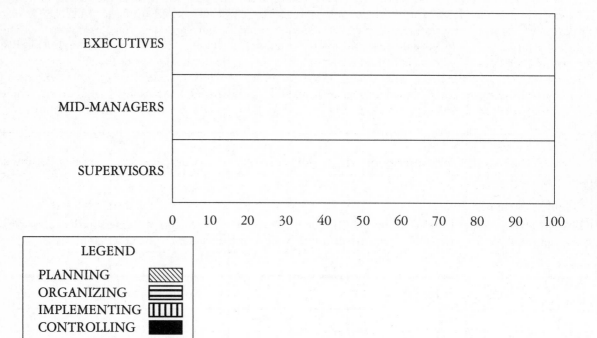

11-B. For each of the following management activities, identify which of the four management functions is being completed. Place the letter of the correct function in the blank beside the item number.

P = Planning
O = Organizing
I = Implementing
C = Controlling

_____ 1. Determining the types of raw materials to use in order to develop a high-quality product.

_____ 2. Completing an employee performance appraisal.

_____ 3. Dividing a large sales territory into two smaller territories and assigning managers and salespeople to the territory.

_____ 4. Deciding if a new product should be added after reviewing test-market results.

5. Discussing a problem with two employees to encourage them to work more closely together rather than continuing to have conflicts.

6. Reviewing the financial statements for the past six months.

7. Deciding to hire an advertising agency to promote a new product because the promotion manager is currently overworked.

8. Conducting a department meeting.

9. Determining salary increases based on annual performance evaluations.

10. Deciding whether to sell stock in the company or borrow money in order to finance a new building.

11-C. You have learned that while supervisors from various companies have many differences in their jobs, they still have a common set of responsibilities. Those common responsibilities are listed in the left column of the following chart. Locate a newspaper that has a large section of classified advertisements for employment or an Internet site that lists employment opportunities. Identify several job announcements for supervisors. Use those advertisements to complete the remaining columns of the chart. For each of the responsibilities listed, (1) identify a part of the job description from one of the advertisements that relates to that responsibility and copy the statement into the second column; (2) copy the job title for that position in the third column; (3) write the name of the company offering the position in the fourth column; and (4) identify the type of business (manufacturer, retailer, etc.) in the last column. Try to identify a different job and company for each of the supervisor responsibilities.

Supervisor Responsibility	Job Description	Job Title	Company	Type of Business
Communicate goals and directions				
Keep management informed				
Evaluate and improve employee performance				
Motivate employees				
Use resources efficiently				

11-D. As a manager of a printing department, you are responsible for scheduling the time of three employees. Each employee works from 9 a.m. until 5 p.m., with lunch from 12:00 until 1:00. You have the following jobs that can be assigned to your employees. All jobs must be assigned.

Job 1	2 hours to complete	must be completed today
Job 2	3½ hours to complete	can be completed tomorrow
Job 3	5½ hours to complete	must be completed today
Job 4	1½ hours to complete	must be completed today
Job 5	3 hours to complete	can be completed tomorrow; cannot be divided
Job 6	4 hours to complete	must be completed today
Job 7	3 hours to complete	must be completed today
Job 8	2½ hours to complete	must be completed today
Job 9	4 hours to complete	can be completed tomorrow
Job 10	2 hours to complete	can be completed tomorrow; cannot be divided

Using the following form, assign the jobs to your three employees. You must make certain that jobs 1, 3, 4, 6, 7, and 8 are done today. Employees should be busy all day, but they cannot begin a job that cannot be completed before 5 p.m. if it is noted that the job cannot be divided.

Time	Day 1			Day 2		
	Employee 1	Employee 2	Employee 3	Employee 1	Employee 2	Employee 3
9:00						
10:00						
11:00						
12:00						
1:00						
2:00						
3:00						
4:00						
5:00						

1. How many hours are your employees available to work during the two-day period?

_____

2. How many hours of jobs did you schedule? _____

3. Based on this information, what problem(s) do you have within your department?

_____

4. Using the decision-making process, define the problem(s) and brainstorm some possible solutions.

_____

_____

_____

11-E. You are the manager of a small gift shop located in a mall. Your store hours are 10:00 a.m. until 9:00 p.m. You typically work during the day with two or three other employees and have a small part-time staff to work the evening hours unsupervised. You receive a monthly projected sales report based on the previous year's sales volume and the season of the year. In reviewing these figures, you have noticed a consistent decline in your sales volume for the last three months. Based on this information, answer the following questions.

1. Is this a symptom or a problem? If this is a symptom, identify at least three possible problems that might be the cause of the symptom.

   _____

   _____

   _____

   _____

2. From your list of possible problems, select one and determine the possible solutions, analyze the solutions, and select the best solution.

   _____

   _____

   _____

   _____

   _____

3. Establish a method to monitor the solution to determine whether or not you have solved the problem.

   _____

   _____

   _____

   _____

SMALL GROUP ACTIVITIES

General Directions

Small groups of three or four students should be created. Each group should be assigned one of the following problems, or the group can select the problem on which the members want to work. Groups should have about 10–15 minutes to discuss the issues and develop answers. When they have completed their activity, the groups should report their answers by recording them on the board, on overhead transparencies, or with presentation software.

Group Activity 1

You are the manager of a kitchen appliance store. For each of the following categories (1) customer needs, (2) competition, and (3) the economy, identify the types of information you need in order to make management decisions about your appliance business. Then develop a procedure for collecting the needed information.

Customer Needs

Competition

Economy

Group Activity 2

You are interested in creating and managing an Internet-based company that allows people to list and resell used music CDs at discounted prices. You will make a profit by charging a fee to the people who list their CDs for resale. Using the four management functions of planning, organizing, implementing, and controlling, list several activities you will need to do under each function.

Planning

Organizing

Implementing

Controlling

Group Activity 3

Imagine you are the principal of your school. A principal is a manager, just like the manager of a business. As your school's principal, list the types of activities you would need to perform under each management function.

Planning

Organizing

Implementing

Controlling

Study Guide

Part A—*Directions:* Indicate your answer to each of the following questions by writing either yes or no in the Answers column.

Answers

1. Do the people who are responsible for an organization need to have leadership skills in order for the organization to be effective? .... 1. _____

2. Do managers today have total authority over the employees in a business? .... 2. _____

3. Does human relations refer to how well people get along together? .... 3. _____

4. Can supervisors get by without leadership skills since they are at the lowest level of management? .... 4. _____

5. Is dependability an important leadership characteristic? .... 5. _____

6. Do effective leaders encourage others to share their ideas, experiences, and opinions? .... 6. _____

7. If a manager is able to get others to do what he or she wants, is that manager an effective leader? .... 7. _____

8. Is position power based on the ability to control resources, rewards, and punishments? .... 8. _____

9. Can a person have power because others identify with and want to be accepted by him or her? .... 9. _____

10. Are managers the only people who have power in an organization? .... 10. _____

11. Do expert and identity power come from a manager's position in the company? .... 11. _____

12. Are human relations skills considered to be as important to the success of a business as the ability to make decisions or operate a complicated piece of equipment? .... 12. _____

13. Should managers treat all employees in the same way? .... 13. _____

14. Should managers attempt to match job tasks with the needs and interests of employees? 14. _____

15. Have studies found that, in general, all employees will not complete work well unless they are closely managed? .... 15. _____

16. Is an autocratic style of leadership most effective when efficiency is important? .... 16. _____

17. Will managers who use a democratic style of leadership generally take more time to make a decision than if another style is used? .... 17. _____

18. Will the open style of leadership work best with inexperienced employees? .... 18. _____

19. Do most management training programs prepare managers to deal with difficult personal problems of their employees? .... 19. _____

20. Do managers who involve employees in developing rules and procedures usually find greater support for those rules and fewer problems when penalties need to be applied for rules violations? .... 20. _____

Total Score   _____

Part B—*Directions:* For each of the following statements, select the word, or group of words, that best completes the statement. In the Answers column, write the letter corresponding to the answer selected.

1. The ability to influence individuals and groups to achieve organizational goals is (a) management, (b) human relations, (c) leadership, (d) none of these. .... 1. _____

2. When leaders have ambition and persistence in reaching goals, they are demonstrating (a) cooperation, (b) initiative, (c) objectivity, (d) stability. .... 2. _____

3. The ability to control behavior in an organization is known as (a) power, (b) leadership, (c) rewards, (d) cooperation. .... 3. _____

4. Expert power is given to people (a) who hold management positions in an organization, (b) who are considered the most knowledgeable, (c) with whom others identify, (d) who do all of these. .... 4. _____

5. The two types of power given to managers by their employees are (a) position and reward, (b) autocratic and democratic, (c) human relations and leadership, (d) expert and identity. 5. _____

6. Which of the following is NOT an important human relations skill needed by managers? (a) self-understanding, (b) communication, (c) developing job satisfaction, (d) judgment. 6. _____

7. Managers who are able to get people to work well together to accomplish the goals of the organization are using which human relations skill? (a) initiative, (b) team-building, (c) power, (d) authority. .... 7. _____

8. Managers who believe employees dislike work are more likely to (a) give employees more responsibility, (b) be effective leaders, (c) use closer supervision and control, (d) have little concern for the quality of employees' work. .... 8. _____

9. Which of the following is a leadership characteristic that employees prefer in their managers? (a) encourages employee participation and questions, (b) informs employees of information only when they need to know, (c) implements few changes, (d) keeps employee training to a minimum. .... 9. _____

10. If a business does not have a formal set of work rules, (a) a union will likely be organized, (b) employees will be highly motivated, (c) managers will receive greater respect from employees, (d) each manager should develop his or her own set of procedures and policies. 10. _____

Total Score _____

Part C—*Directions:* In the Answers column, write the letter of the word or expression in Column I that most closely matches each statement in Column II.

Column I	Column II	Answers
A. open leader	1. Encourages workers to share in making decisions about work-related problems	_____
B. democratic leader		
C. autocratic leader	2. The ability of an employee's boss to give directions and expect the employee to complete the work	_____
D. leadership	3. The ability to influence individuals and groups to achieve organizational goals	_____
E. position power	4. Gives direct, clear, and precise orders with detailed instructions	_____
	5. Gives little or no direction to others	_____
	Total Score	_____

Name _____

Directions: Study each controversial issue carefully. Follow the advice of your teacher before listing in the columns provided reasons why people might answer Yes or No. Your teacher may want you to work with a classmate, talk with others in your community to gather information, or use the library or Internet to gather facts.

12-1. Do all managers in an organization need effective leadership skills in order for the organization to be successful?

Reasons for "Yes"	Reasons for "No"

12-2. Do you believe some people are "natural leaders"? That is, they need little or no leadership training, while other people will never be leaders no matter how much training they receive.

Reasons for "Yes"	Reasons for "No"

PROBLEMS

12-A. Studies of leaders have found that most effective leaders share common personal characteristics. It is possible to determine if you have those characteristics and to develop a personal plan to improve those characteristics that are not as strong as you would like. You can evaluate your leadership characteristics by answering the following questions. For each question, insert a check mark in the appropriate column. Questions that you answer "always" or "usually" indicate areas where you already have developed leadership skills. The areas where you answer "sometimes" or "never" indicate traits you will need to improve if you are to become a more effective leader.

	Always	Usually	Sometimes	Never
1. Do you perform above average in your classes in school? ...	_____	_____	_____	_____
2. Do you enjoy making decisions?	_____	_____	_____	_____
3. Do your parents and friends trust your judgment?	_____	_____	_____	_____
4. Are you able to put your personal feelings aside when you have to make important decisions?	_____	_____	_____	_____
5. Do you take time to gather information before you draw conclusions?	_____	_____	_____	_____
6. Do you look forward to starting new tasks?	_____	_____	_____	_____
7. When you face a challenge, do you keep working until you find a solution?	_____	_____	_____	_____
8. Can people depend on you to do what you say you will do?	_____	_____	_____	_____
9. Are you involved in team sports and group activities?	_____	_____	_____	_____
10. Do you prefer working with others rather than alone?	_____	_____	_____	_____
11. Are you upset when you see others being dishonest?	_____	_____	_____	_____
12. Are you willing to say no to your friends when they ask you to do things you disagree with?	_____	_____	_____	_____
13. Do you prefer to find new ways to do routine activities rather than continuing to do them the same way?	_____	_____	_____	_____
14. When you have to do something you have never done before, do you believe you will be successful?	_____	_____	_____	_____
15. When you are in a difficult situation, do you remain calm?	_____	_____	_____	_____
16. Do you listen to the concerns and problems of your friends more often than you tell them about yourself?	_____	_____	_____	_____
17. When working in a group, do you encourage everyone to participate and contribute?	_____	_____	_____	_____
18. Do you have friends who have different backgrounds and interests than you?	_____	_____	_____	_____
19. Do you respect the feelings and beliefs of others, even if you do not agree with them?	_____	_____	_____	_____
20. When you are in situations where you don't know other people, do you take the initiative to get to know them?	_____	_____	_____	_____

12-B. For each of the following items, indicate whether the manager was using an autocratic, democratic, or open style of leadership by placing a check mark in the appropriate column.

	Autocratic	Democratic	Open
1. Each worker is allowed to decide how his or her job will be done.	_____	_____	_____
2. An employee meeting is held each week to discuss problems. ..	_____	_____	_____
3. The manager lets employees cooperatively decide when breaks should be scheduled.	_____	_____	_____
4. There are no work rules for the department.	_____	_____	_____
5. Before changing an evaluation system, the manager explained to the employees why it was being changed.	_____	_____	_____
6. The manager tells each new employee how the job should be done.	_____	_____	_____
7. When two employees had an argument, the manager told them how to solve their problem.	_____	_____	_____
8. The store owner lets department managers order any merchandise they choose.	_____	_____	_____
9. The store owner sets all department budgets.	_____	_____	_____
10. The manager conducts an employee brainstorming session to develop a new advertising slogan.	_____	_____	_____

12-C. The marketing manager for a manufacturing firm has been given the task of selecting new automobiles for ten of the company's salespeople. The company has lease agreements with dealers representing three brands of automobiles. The manager knows that each salesperson has personal preferences about the brand, model, and options in an automobile. The company also will save money if all of the cars are leased from the same dealer and even more money if all cars are the same model with the same options.

For each of the three leadership styles, describe how the manager would make the decision on the automobiles to purchase. Then list one advantage and one disadvantage of the use of that leadership style in this situation.

Autocratic Style: _____

_____

Advantage: _____

Disadvantage: _____

Democratic Style: _____

_____

Advantage: _____

Disadvantage: _____

Open Style: _____

_____

Advantage: _____

Disadvantage: _____

12-D. A recent survey of 150 employees with five or more years of experience asked the employees to identify the type of leadership style they preferred from their supervisors. The following results were obtained: Autocratic—38 employees; Democratic—66 employees; Open—22 employees; Combination of styles—24 employees.

1. In the space below, construct a pie chart showing the percentage of employees preferring each type of leadership style.

Employees' Preferred Leadership Styles

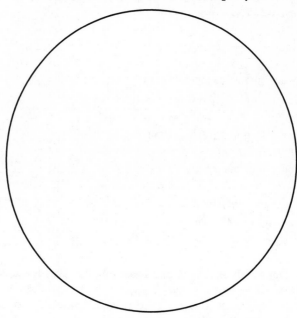

2. In the space below, identify the leadership style you would prefer from a supervisor and the reasons for your preference. _____

_____

_____

_____

3. Why do you believe employees prefer very different leadership styles? How can a manager respond when his or her employees work best under different leadership styles? _____

_____

_____

_____

_____

12-E. Work rules are developed to create and maintain an effective work environment and to help employees work efficiently. In the space below, write two work rules for you and the other students in your class. Also write a sentence that describes why you believe the rule would result in an effective work atmosphere in the class and would help students work more efficiently. After you finish writing your statements, the other students in the class will vote on each statement. The vote will determine whether they agree that each of your rules would help to maintain an effective and efficient working atmosphere.

Work Rule #1: _____

_____

_____

Justification: _____

_____

_____

Student Vote: Agree _____ Disagree _____

Work Rule #2: _____

_____

_____

Justification: _____

_____

_____

Student Vote: Agree _____ Disagree _____

SMALL GROUP ACTIVITIES

Group Activity 1

With instructions from your teacher, divide into small groups of four or five students. Review the list of leadership characteristics in Figure 12-1 of your text. As a group, choose five people, either living or dead, who exhibit(ed) an excellent leadership style and give the reasons for your choices. Using presentation software, prepare your answers for presentation to the class.

Group Activity 2

This group activity will take more than one class period and involves an interview with a businessperson during nonschool time.

With instructions from your teacher, divide into small groups of four or five students. With your group, brainstorm a list of questions to ask a businessperson about management styles, leadership styles, employee management techniques, and employee work groups. Individually or in pairs, interview a businessperson, using your questions as a basis for the interview. When all group members have completed their interviews, meet with your group and share your information. Your teacher might ask you to summarize your information and prepare it in either written form or for an oral presentation to the class.

<table>
<tr><td rowspan="3">Chapter 13

Planning and Organizing</td><td rowspan="3">Name _____

Date _____</td><td colspan="5" align="center">Scoring Record</td></tr>
<tr><td></td><td>Part A</td><td>Part B</td><td>Part C</td><td>Total</td></tr>
<tr><td>Perfect score</td><td>20</td><td>10</td><td>5</td><td>35</td></tr>
<tr><td colspan="2"></td><td>My score</td><td></td><td></td><td></td><td></td></tr>
</table>

Study Guide

Part A—*Directions:* Indicate your answer to each of the following questions by writing either yes or no in the Answers column.

Answers

1. Should a business plan include a detailed financial analysis showing the potential profitability of the firm? .... 1. _____
2. Are all business managers involved in planning in some way? .... 2. _____
3. Do plans serve as guides for decision making? .... 3. _____
4. Does planning usually result in more communication and coordination problems in the business? .... 4. _____
5. Is long-term planning that provides broad goals and directions for the entire business known as operational planning? .... 5. _____
6. Is the development of a business plan an example of strategic planning? .... 6. _____
7. Is external analysis the first step in strategic planning? .... 7. _____
8. Are supervisors usually responsible for strategic planning? .... 8. _____
9. Does operational planning include decisions about the resources that will be needed to get the work done in a specific area of the business? .... 9. _____
10. Are goals statements of the results that a business expects to achieve? .... 10. _____
11. Is it better for goals to be general rather than specific? .... 11. _____
12. Does a schedule include both the identification of tasks to be completed and the time needed to complete each task? .... 12. _____
13. Is a schedule a measure against which something is judged? .... 13. _____
14. Is a policy more specific than a procedure? .... 14. _____
15. Does an organizational chart show the reporting relationships among the organization's personnel? .... 15. _____
16. As a business grows, does the number of major divisions in the organization usually decrease? .... 16. _____
17. Is authority the obligation to do an assigned task? .... 17. _____
18. In an effective organization, do most employees have more than one supervisor from whom they receive job assignments? .... 18. _____
19. In general, is the span of control larger at the lower levels of an organization than at the higher levels? .... 19. _____
20. Is the most flexible type of organizational structure the matrix organization? .... 20. _____

Total Score _____

Part B—*Directions:* For each of the following statements, select the word, or group of words, that best completes the statement. In the Answers column, write the letter corresponding to the answer selected.

1. Which of the following would NOT be a part of strategic planning? (a) mission statement, (b) goals, (c) strategies, (d) department work assignments. .... 1. _____

2. To be effective, goals should be (a) general rather than specific, (b) slightly higher than can be realistically achieved, (c) independent from all other goals, (d) meaningful. .... 2. _____

3. One type of financial planning tool is a (a) goal, (b) budget, (c) standard, (d) schedule. .... 3. _____

4. Guidelines used in making decisions regarding specific, recurring situations are known as (a) policies, (b) procedures, (c) standards, (d) goals. .... 4. _____

5. The management function responsible for arranging resources and relationships between departments and employees and defining the responsibility each has for accomplishing the job is (a) planning, (b) organizing, (c) implementing, (d) controlling. .... 5. _____

6. A visual device that shows the structure of an organization and the relationships among workers and divisions of work is (a) a schedule, (b) a strategic plan, (c) an organization chart, (d) an operational plan. .... 6. _____

7. Companies that have started using work teams and that involve employees in planning and decision making have found that span of control (a) must be decreased, (b) can be increased, (c) is no longer needed, (d) is not affected. .... 7. _____

8. The organization in which all authority and responsibility can be traced directly from the top executive to the lowest employee level is the (a) line organization, (b) line-and-staff organization, (c) matrix organization, (d) decentralized organization. .... 8. _____

9. Specialists are available to give advice and assistance to managers in the (a) line organization, (b) line-and-staff organization, (c) matrix organization, (d) decentralized organization. 9. _____

10. A few top managers do all major planning and decision making in a (a) line organization, (b) line-and-staff organization, (c) centralized organization, (d) decentralized organization. 10. _____

Total Score _____

Part C—*Directions:* Complete each sentence by filling in the missing word or words.

1. _____ to make decisions about work assignments is delegated from the _____ of the organization to the _____ of the organization.

2. Accountability is the obligation to accept responsibility for the _____ of assigned tasks, including the _____, _____, and completion time.

3. _____ _____ _____ requires that no employee have more than one supervisor at a time.

4. Span of control refers to the _____ of employees who are directly _____ by one person.

5. A project or matrix organization combines workers into temporary _____ _____ to complete a specific project, and a project _____ has the authority and responsibility for the project.

Total Score _____

Name _____

Directions: Study each controversial issue carefully. Follow the advice of your teacher before listing in the columns provided reasons why people might answer Yes or No. Your teacher may want you to work with a class-mate, talk with others in your community to gather information, or use the library or Internet to gather facts.

13-1. Do you believe that long-range plans should be developed in businesses where economic conditions and competition are changing very rapidly?

Reasons for "Yes"	Reasons for "No"

13-2. Do you believe most businesses would be more successful if they used a project or matrix organizational structure rather than a line or a line-and-staff organizational structure?

Reasons for "Yes"	Reasons for "No"

PROBLEMS

13-A. Classify each of the following activities of a business as either strategic planning or operational planning by placing a check mark in the appropriate column.

Business Activity	Strategic Planning	Operational Planning
1. A new warehouse will be built to serve the markets in the northeast section of the country.	_____	_____
2. The advertising budget for the next three months will be increased by 2 percent to attract more customers into the store.	_____	_____
3. The Cleveland facility will schedule a one-week shutdown in December to allow for equipment repairs.	_____	_____
4. An export office in Rome will be used to develop plans for European market development.	_____	_____
5. A small business owner has decided to expand into other states by selling franchises.	_____	_____
6. Employees will be asked to work three hours of overtime each week to meet the increased summer demand.	_____	_____

13-B. Business goals must be specific and meaningful in order to be useful to managers and employers. Each of the following statements is very general, but can be used as a basis for developing a goal for the business. Rewrite each statement to make it an effective goal.

1. The men's shoe department needs to increase its sales volume.

_____

_____

2. Too many radios produced on the third shift are defective and have to be discarded.

_____

_____

3. We've seen an increase in employee turnover since January.

_____

_____

4. We would like to increase the amount each customer spends when he or she shops in our Westgate store.

_____

_____

Name _____

13-C. A well-developed procedure for completing a task can be an effective tool to help a new employee learn a job. However, it is not easy to develop a procedure that includes every necessary step. In the space below, write the steps of the procedure someone should follow to accurately write a check. To determine if the procedure works, have another student follow the steps exactly to fill out the blank check shown below. When the student is finished, evaluate the work to see if it has been done correctly.

_____
_____
_____
_____
_____
_____
_____
_____

N.E. Name
33 Your Street
Anytown, U.S. 11223

_____

_____ 20 _____ 72-7073/2739

PAY TO THE
ORDER OF _____ $ _____

_____ DOLLARS

THE FIRST NATIONAL BANK
ANYTOWN, U.S. 11223

FOR CLASSROOM USE ONLY

MEMO _____ _____

|:27390734|:

13-D. Your school requires all students to complete 100 hours of community service in order to be eligible for graduation. As the president of a high school club, you have decided to start an after-school reading and math tutoring program at an area middle school to help your club members earn the necessary volunteer hours. You and the other club officers want to establish policies regarding this program before you take your suggestion to the middle school principal for approval. Write at least five policies regarding this new tutoring program.
(Suggestions: attendance, dress, conduct, transportation, hours, academic performance, recommendations.)

_____
_____
_____
_____
_____
_____

13-E. The most common type of organizational structure in a large business is the line-and-staff organization. In such an organization, the staff person investigates problems and consults with and advises line administrators. The line administrators determine policies and procedures and give orders for carrying out their decisions.

The organizational information below describes ten positions within a company, whether they are line or staff positions, and their responsibilities. After reviewing the information, draw a line-and-staff organizational chart in the space provided, showing the relationships between the ten positions.

	Position	Line or Staff	Responsibilities
1.	President	line	Directs the company
2.	Vice president of manufacturing	line	Reports to the president
3.	Company attorney	staff	Reports to the president and advises the vice presidents of manufacturing and sales
4.	Chemist who tests raw materials purchased	staff	Reports to the vice president of manufacturing and advises the manufacturing and production managers
5.	District sales manager	line	Reports to the vice president of sales
6.	Advertising specialist	staff	Reports to the vice president of sales and works with sales management
7.	Superintendent of manufacturing	line	Reports to the vice president of manufacturing
8.	Supervisor of production	line	Reports to the superintendent of manufacturing
9.	Vice president of sales	line	Reports to the president
10.	Personnel manager	staff	Reports to the president and works with the vice presidents of manufacturing and sales

Name _____

Line-and-Staff Organizational Chart

SMALL GROUP ACTIVITIES

You are a member of the Leadership Club, which has decided to hold a pre-prom fashion show during your school's lunch periods. Your club will collaborate with three major department stores in a nearby mall and two tuxedo rental stores. In addition, area florists and restaurants are interested in setting up booths during the same lunch periods to advertise their merchandise and services.

Group Activity 1

With instructions from your teacher, divide into groups of four or five students. In your group, develop a strategic plan for the fashion show, including goals and operational plans showing a timeline and identifying the people responsible for each activity.

Group Activity 2

Create an organizational chart for the pre-prom fashion show. You can choose a line, line-and-staff, matrix, or work-team structure to accomplish your goals. Develop a written justification for your choice of organizational structure.

Study Guide

Part A—*Directions:* Indicate your answer to each of the following questions by writing either yes or no in the Answers column.

Answers

1. Are plans likely to be ineffective if they are not implemented well? .... 1. _____

2. Does implementing involve guiding employee work toward achieving the company's goals? .... 2. _____

3. Are all rewards motivating? .... 3. _____

4. Is employee motivation influenced by both internal and external factors? .... 4. _____

5. Is there a positive relationship between an employee's need satisfaction and motivation? 5. _____

6. Will each member of a work team usually be working to achieve different goals? .... 6. _____

7. Are operations the major ongoing activities of a business? .... 7. _____

8. Is process improvement the efforts to increase the effectiveness and efficiency of specific business operations? .... 8. _____

9. Is self-actualization the lowest level on Maslow's hierarchy of needs? .... 9. _____

10. Is McClelland's achievement motivation theory based on a belief that people are influenced most strongly by a need for power, affiliation, or achievement? .... 10. _____

11. Do the hygiene factors identified by Fredrick Herzberg motivate employees? .... 11. _____

12. In Herzberg's theory of motivation, do the same factors provide both satisfaction and dissatisfaction for people? .... 12. _____

13. Do people usually accept change easily? .... 13. _____

14. Is it usually best for managers to say nothing to employees about possible changes until a final decision has been made? .... 14. _____

15. To make changes effectively, should managers provide information and training to employees? .... 15. _____

16. Does the controlling process include measuring performance? .... 16. _____

17. Would the minimum number of units to be produced in a day be an example of a quantity standard? .... 17. _____

18. Is increasing sales the only way a business can increase its profits? .... 18. _____

19. Can a variance be positive or negative? .... 19. _____

20. Should managers ever change the standard if a business is not meeting the standard that was set? .... 20. _____

Total Score _____

Part B—*Directions:* For each of the following statements, select the word, or group of words, that best completes the statement. In the Answers column, write the letter corresponding to the answer selected.

Answers

1. The set of factors that influence an individual's actions toward accomplishing a goal is (a) management, (b) effective communication, (c) control, (d) motivation. .... 1. _____

2. A group of individuals who cooperate to achieve a common goal is (a) a supervisory group, (b) an employee group, (c) a work team, (d) a grapevine. .... 2. _____

3. The motivation theory based on a progression through five categories of need was developed by (a) Herzberg, (b) Maslow, (c) McClelland, (d) Taylor. .... 3. _____

4. According to McClelland, people who want to influence and control others have (a) an achievement need, (b) an affiliation need, (c) a power need, (d) all of these needs. .... 4. _____

5. Motivators are to hygiene factors as (a) Herzberg is to Maslow, (b) basic needs are to affiliation needs, (c) recognition is to achievement, (d) recognition is to working conditions. 5. _____

6. Which of the following is an important step in effective change? (a) Move rapidly to implement the change. (b) Delay communications about the change until decisions have been made. (c) Involve the people affected in making decisions about the change. (d) Avoid offering too much support as people adjust to the change. .... 6. _____

7. Which of the following is NOT a part of the controlling process? (a) establishing standards, (b) motivating employees, (c) measuring and comparing performance, (d) taking corrective action. .... 7. _____

8. When performance is lower than the standard, it means (a) the company will probably not be able to perform at the expected level, (b) there are problems between planning and implementing activities, (c) managers need to take corrective action soon, (d) all of these. 8. _____

9. A just-in-time control system would be most useful for managing (a) inventory, (b) credit, (c) theft, (d) none of these. .... 9. _____

10. On average, the percentage of total sales lost each year by retailers to theft from customers and employees is (a) almost nothing, (b) 1–2%, (c) 6%, (d) 15%. .... 10. _____

Total Score _____

Part C—*Directions:* In the Answers column, write the letter of the word or expression in Column I that most closely matches each statement in Column II.

Column I	Column II	Answers
A. implementing	1. Determining if goals are being met and the actions needed if they are not.	_____
B. controlling	2. Two-factor theory of motivation.	_____
C. Herzberg	3. People's behavior is most strongly influenced by one of three needs: power, affiliation, or achievement.	_____
D. McClelland	4. Carrying out plans and helping employees to work effectively.	_____
E. Maslow	5. People are motivated by five levels of needs, beginning with physiological needs.	_____
	Total Score	_____

116

Directions: Study each controversial issue carefully. Follow the advice of your teacher before listing in the columns provided reasons why people might answer Yes or No. Your teacher may want you to work with a classmate, talk with others in your community to gather information, or use the library or Internet to gather facts.

14-1. Even if a business is operating effectively and profitably, should the company's managers be planning for and implementing changes?

Reasons for "Yes"	Reasons for "No"

14-2. Do you agree with Herzberg's theory of motivation that the absence of good pay, benefits, and working conditions can dissatisfy employees, but the presence of these factors cannot satisfy them?

Reasons for "Yes"	Reasons for "No"

PROBLEMS

14-A. Effective teams can make the difference between success and failure in a business, an athletic event, a class project, a club, or other group activity. Using your own experience, identify one team or work group you have been a part of that you considered to be effective and one that you considered to be ineffective. Complete the following chart, describing your view of each of the teams. Then answer the questions that follow the chart.

	Effective Team	Ineffective Team
Characteristics		
Description of the team		
Purpose of the team		
Did team members support the team's purpose?		
Did each member understand his/her responsibilities?		
Were all members committed to the group?		
Were the activities to be completed clear?		
Did members have the needed skills for success?		
Did members communicate effectively?		
Did members work to solve problems?		

1. Did the characteristics of the team appear to affect whether the group was successful or not?

   _____

2. Which of the characteristics seemed to be most important to the group's success?

   _____

3. Which of the characteristics seemed to contribute to group's problems?

   _____

4. If you were helping to organize a new group or team, what would you do to try to make it more effective in achieving its goals? _____

14-B. Each of the following statements describes a principle of motivation. Read each statement and then select the theory that includes the principle by placing a check mark in the appropriate column.

Principle of Motivation	Maslow	Herzberg	McClelland
1. People must satisfy their security needs before social needs motivate their behavior.	____	____	____
2. The highest level of need is self-actualization.	____	____	____
3. Managers working with individuals with a high achievement need should provide opportunities for them to make decisions and control their own work.	____	____	____
4. Two distinct factors contribute to employee satisfaction or dissatisfaction.	____	____	____
5. A person with a power need wants to control and influence people.	____	____	____
6. Until physiological needs are satisfied, people will be concerned about little else.	____	____	____
7. Pay increases will prevent employees from being dissatisfied but will not motivate them to better performance.	____	____	____
8. One group of workers will take personal responsibility for their work, while another group will be more concerned about getting along.	____	____	____
9. Great motivators are challenging work, recognition, and personal development.	____	____	____

14-C. Hasme Manufacturing, Inc., produces small components for computer systems. Quality control is very important, so each product is carefully tested when it is completed. If the product does not meet quality standards, it is rejected and returned for improvement. Management is also concerned that quantity standards are maintained so that orders are filled on schedule.

Jan Rankin, vice president of manufacturing, has collected information on production levels for four weeks. The production for each day of the week was totaled during the four-week period. The chart below shows the total number of items produced and the total number rejected for each day of the week for four weeks.

	Monday	Tuesday	Wednesday	Thursday	Friday
Total Parts Produced	1,480	1,500	1,520	1,550	1,460
Total Parts Rejected	172	140	125	111	169

1. On which day of the week were the most acceptable components produced? _____

2. On which day were the fewest acceptable components produced? _____

3. How many parts were produced on an average workday at the Hasme Manufacturing? _____

4. How many parts were rejected on an average workday? _____

5. Using the information in the chart above, construct a bar graph on the form on the next page. The graph should show the percentage of component parts rejected for each day of the week.

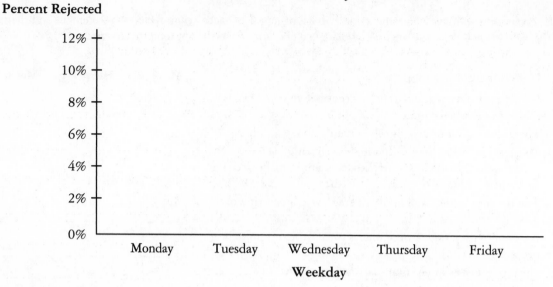

COMPONENT PART REJECTION RATE

Percent Rejected

12%

10%

8%

6%

4%

2%

0%

Monday   Tuesday   Wednesday   Thursday   Friday

Weekday

14-D. The following chart shows the projected and actual sales for several models of televisions in an appliance store. Complete the chart by calculating the amount the actual sales varied from the budgeted amounts. Next, calculate the percentage of variance from projected sales for each item. Finally, determine the total variance between projected and actual sales and the percentage of variance between planned and actual sales.

Model No.	Projected Sales	Actual Sales	Variance	Percentage Variance
XTL-13	$ 11,325	$ 13,250	_____	_____
ZT-13	11,985	9,995	_____	_____
XTL-15	12,840	10,620	_____	_____
ZT-15	13,825	15,385	_____	_____
MG-19	11,540	11,540	_____	_____
RC-19	12,650	9,985	_____	_____
MG-25	19,020	21,855	_____	_____
RC-25	20,330	20,960	_____	_____
MB-45	13,790	15,015	_____	_____
Totals	_____	_____	_____	_____

14-E. A company that manufactures bicycles received an order from a national sporting goods chain. The order was for 150 bicycles that must be manufactured in 30 days. After 10 days, 45 bicycles had been produced. The manager scheduled the employees to work overtime for two Saturdays. At the end of 20 days, 110 bicycles were completed.

1. Write a standard for daily bicycle production that the company must meet in order to complete the order in the required 30 days. _____

2. At the end of the first 10 days, what was the total variance from the number of bicycles that should have been completed? _____

3. What was the variance from the daily standard at the end of the first ten days? _____

_____

_____

4. What was the corrective action taken by the manager? _____

_____

5. At the end of 20 days, what was the total variance from the number of bicycles that should have been completed? _____

_____

6. Write a standard for the daily production of bicycles for the last 10 days in order to complete the contract on schedule. _____

_____

7. What should the manager do if the production level exceeds the standard during the first two of the remaining production days? _____

_____

_____

_____

SMALL GROUP ACTIVITIES

Group Activity 1

With instructions from your teacher, divide into groups of four or five students. In your group, read the following scenario and complete the activity.

You have recently purchased a medium-sized wholesale florist shop from the original owner and are now the owner/manager. You know the business has many dedicated employees who have been with the company for years. The shop has been in business in the same community since the 1960s, and while it is successful, many of its operations are quite out-of-date. For example, all business records—including purchasing, accounting, shipping, and receiving—are still maintained manually. You have contracted with a computer software company to develop a computerized system for your entire operation. The system is now ready to be implemented. You are sure that many of your employees will resist the change.

 Using what you have learned about managing change, develop a list of procedures you will follow to prepare the employees for the change and successfully implement the new computerized system.

Group Activity 2

With instructions from your teacher, divide into groups of four or five students. In your group, read the following scenario and complete the activity.

Raoul Estevez, the manager of The Corner Eatery, a medium-sized family restaurant, has recently been experiencing declining sales and customer complaints about poor service. In addition, his wait staff has been complaining about reduced tips, and several have indicated they are considering looking for new jobs at other restaurants. Mr. Estevez is considering raising prices to counteract the declining sales but does not know what to do about the poor-service complaints. In the past, his management style was to immediately and publicly reprimand employees to motivate them when he saw a performance problem.

 Your group represents a management consulting firm. Mr. Estevez has decided to ask your firm to make recommendations to correct the problems in his restaurant. Drawing on information from the chapter regarding implementing and controlling, policy change, motivating employees, and setting standards, develop a plan for Mr. Estevez to correct the problems he is experiencing in his restaurant.

Study Guide

Part A—*Directions:* Indicate your answer to each of the following questions by writing either yes or no in the Answers column.

Answers

1. Are financial records summaries of a business's financial activities and information? .... 1. _____

2. Is outsourcing usually more expensive than hiring someone into the business who has the needed expertise? .... 2. _____

3. Do data processing centers prepare and maintain a full set of financial records for other businesses? .... 3. _____

4. With a point-of sale-terminal, is each item that is sold automatically subtracted from the recorded inventory so the computer can calculate when the store needs to reorder merchandise? .... 4. _____

5. Do accounts receivable records show the money that businesses owe and payments they make to purchase supplies and merchandise on credit? .... 5. _____

6. Are tools and computers used in a business's operations examples of assets? .... 6. _____

7. Is an employer required to keep complete payroll records that show the hours worked, regular wages paid, overtime wages, and all types of deductions from wages for each employee? .... 7. _____

8. Should all critical records of a business such as leases and contracts be kept on site to offer the greatest protection from loss or damage? .... 8. _____

9. Are budgets based on actual costs rather than on projections? .... 9. _____

10. Does an operating budget project income and expenses from the beginning of a new business until it becomes profitable? .... 10. _____

11. Do managers often prepare three budget estimates rather than relying on just one? .... 11. _____

12. Are financial statements estimates of a business's financial performance for a specific period of time in the future? .... 12. _____

13. Are assets and capital the only categories listed on the balance sheet? .... 13. _____

14. Is the basic accounting equation represented on the balance sheet as Assets = Liabilities + Capital? .... 14. _____

15. Can a business determine whether it can pay all its debts on a given date from looking at the income statement? .... 15. _____

16. Does the difference between total revenue and total expenses show the profit or loss of a business? .... 16. _____

17. Does money usually flow into and out of a business at the same rate? .... 17. _____

18. Is the amount of working capital one possible indicator that a business can pay its long-term debts? .... 18. _____

19. Would a business with very little working capital find it easy to borrow money? .... 19. _____

20. Can a financial ratio show whether the average monthly inventory might be too large or too small? .... 20. _____

Total Score _____

Part B—*Directions:* For each of the following statements, select the word, or group of words, that best completes the statement. In the Answers column, write the letter corresponding to the answer selected.

1. What type of record shows what each customer owes and pays? (a) accounts receivable record, (b) accounts payable record, (c) asset record, (d) depreciation record. .... 1. _____

2. Because of depreciation, (a) the company's equipment will be worth more next year than it is today, (b) the company's equipment will be worth less next year than it is today, (c) the company must buy more equipment than it needs, (d) the company cannot determine the current value of older equipment. .... 2. _____

3. Which fixed asset is LEAST likely to lose its value over time? (a) land, (b) equipment, (c) buildings, (d) a newly purchased delivery van. .... 3. _____

4. A digital video player becomes inadequate because a better type of technology comes on the market. What term describes this example? (a) asset book value, (b) depreciation, (c) replacement value, (d) obsolescence. .... 4. _____

5. A budget is used by management for each of the following EXCEPT to (a) set financial goals, (b) develop operating plans, (c) keep expenses in line with income, (d) determine the amount of profit the business will actually receive. .... 5. _____

6. A sales budget is (a) a report of the actual sales for the last year, (b) a report of inventory on hand that is ready to be sold, (c) an estimate of the sales for the next month or year, (d) a report of the actual sales of each salesperson, product, or sales territory. .... 6. _____

7. A financial plan for replacing fixed assets or acquiring new ones is (a) a capital budget, (b) an operating plan, (c) a startup budget, (d) a balance sheet. .... 7. _____

8. Which of the following is NOT a result of the use of budgets and budgeting systems? (a) It helps reduce losses and increase profits. (b) It improves planning and controlling operations. (c) It improves the accuracy of future budgets. (d) All are results of using budgets and budgeting systems. .... 8. _____

9. On which financial statement does a business list the building in which it does business? (a) balance sheet, (b) asset statement, (c) income statement, (d) cash flow statement. .... 9. _____

10. After subtracting liabilities from assets, a business can determine (a) income for the period, (b) how much it owes, (c) how much it is worth, (d) the total amount of expenses. 10. _____

11. The balance sheet reveals the basic financial position of a business (a) on a given date, (b) for a month, (c) for a year, (d) for whatever time period is specified. .... 11. _____

12. Another name for an income statement is (a) net worth, (b) profit and loss statement (c) owner's equity, (d) statement of financial position. .... 12. _____

13. Which of the following can be determined from a business's income statement? (a) accounts payable, (b) assets, (c) operating expenses, (d) capital. .... 13. _____

14. The difference between current assets and current liabilities is (a) profit, (b) working capital, (c) net worth, (d) net loss. .... 14. _____

15. An agency of the federal government that can assist new and small firms in obtaining credit and other financial support is the (a) Federal Trade Commission, (b) Internal Revenue Service, (c) New Business Support Agency, (d) Small Business Administration. .... 15. _____

Total Score _____

Directions: Study each controversial issue carefully. Follow the advice of your teacher before listing in the columns provided reasons why people might answer Yes or No. Your teacher may want you to work with a class-mate, talk with others in your community to gather information, or use the library or Internet to gather facts.

15-1. Should the budgets developed during the first years of a new business be given limited attention because they take valuable time to analyze that can be used for other important tasks, are usually not very accurate, and seldom recognize important changes that affect the business's financial performance?

Reasons for "Yes"	Reasons for "No"

15-2. To reduce the failure rate of businesses as well as increase the confidence of investors and customers, should each profit-making organization, whether large or small, be required yearly to hire a CPA to approve the financial records of the business?

Reasons for "Yes"	Reasons for "No"

PROBLEMS

15-A. London's Market is a small grocery store where you are employed. For each business practice, indicate by a check mark in the columns at the right whether they are good or bad practices for the safe handling of cash.

		Good	Bad
1.	Any cash in denominations of twenty dollars or less is left in the cash registers at the end of each day to be used as the next day's change fund.	_____	_____
2.	Cashiers are allowed to make change from the cash registers if needed for their personal use.	_____	_____
3.	Deposits are made twice daily in a nearby bank within an hour after two assistant managers collect, count, and verify the amounts from each cash register.	_____	_____
4.	Small payments of under $20 are made from a petty cash fund which is maintained by the bookkeeper who records all cash deposits and withdrawals as they are made from the fund.	_____	_____
5.	Full-time personnel are paid by check, but part-time workers can receive cash if they request it.	_____	_____

15-B. Businesses must maintain many different records. Below are listed some of those records and the average time such records are kept by many firms. Study the information and answer the questions that follow.

1. Which type of business record is kept the shortest time? _____

2. Which two records are kept indefinitely? _____

3. Name three types of records that are retained for only five years.

   _____

4. What problems might a business face when many records are maintained for long periods of time?

   _____

   _____

   _____

   _____

15-C. Brian Douglas maintains a number of the soft drink vending machines in a business's cafeteria. Each day he is responsible for determining the value of the inventory sold, removing coins from the machines, counting the cash collected, and calculating the daily gross profit earned from the machines. Use the information below to determine the amount of cash taken in today from the number of coins removed from the machines.

Nickels	708	$ _____
Dimes	1,146	$ _____
Quarters	3,026	$ _____
Half-dollars	42	$ _____
Total cash		$ _____

Brian replaced 742 bottles of soft drinks that had been sold. The cost of each bottle is 63 cents. Calculate the following values based on income and expenses.

Total cost of inventory sold $ _____

Gross profit $ _____

List some expenses that Brian must calculate in order to determine the net profit earned from the vending machines.

_____

_____

_____

15-D. From the following data, prepare an estimate of cash needs on the form provided for the month of May: expected sales in May, $45,000; expected collections from customers, $39,000; beginning cash balance, $8,250; ending cash balance desired, $6,000; estimated payments—accounts to be paid, $30,600; salaries and wages, $11,000; other operating expenses, $4,000; purchase of display cases, $2,400.

Estimate of Cash Needs, Month of May, 20- -		
Beginning cash balance	(1)	$ _____
Collections from customers	(2)	_____
Total cash available	(3)	$ _____
Payments:		
Accounts to be paid	(4)	$ _____
Salaries and wages	(5)	_____
Other operating expenses	(6)	_____
Purchase of fixed assets	(7)	_____
Total payments	(8)	$ _____
Expected cash shortage	(9)	$ _____
Bank loans needed	(10)	_____
Desired ending cash balance	(11)	$ _____

15-E. A manufacturing firm has four new pieces of equipment. Determine the depreciation expense for the first year of use from the following information:

Equipment	Price	Expected Life	Final Trade-In Value	First Year's Depreciation
A	$160,000	36 months	$10,000	$ _____
B	$ 88,400	60 months	$ -0-	$ _____
C	$754,000	54 months	$14,000	$ _____
D	$ 930	30 months	$ 100	$ _____

15-F. Make the necessary calculations to complete the following expense report for a business. Then answer the questions:

	Budgeted Amount	Actual Amount	Difference
Production costs	$ 370,000	$ 287,000	$ _____
Salaries	150,000	185,000	_____
Depreciation	30,000	30,000	_____
Electricity	5,000	6,500	_____
Supplies	4,000	2,600	_____
Total expenses	$ _____	$ _____	$ _____

1. Do you feel the manager did an effective job in preparing the total budgeted amount?

   Yes _____   No _____

   Justify your decision:

   _____

   _____

   _____

2. What are possible reasons that the budgeted amount for production costs is so much greater than the actual amount?

   _____

   _____

   _____

   _____

   _____

3. What are possible reasons why the actual amount for salaries is so much greater than the budgeted amount?

_____

_____

_____

_____

4. Why might it be wise for the manager to prepare three different budget estimates?

_____

_____

_____

_____

15-G. From the information provided, prepare a balance sheet using the form that follows. Data needed: cash on hand, $48,500; customers owe the business, $16,400; goods bought and ready to be sold, $97,000; equipment, $100,000; buildings and land, $620,000; money owed other businesses, $64,300; and money owed on buildings and land, $208,000.

THE OWL OUTLET

_____

_____

Assets		Liabilities & Capital	
_____	$ _____	Liabilities:	
_____	_____	_____	
_____	_____	_____	$ _____
_____	_____	_____	_____
_____	_____	Total Liabilities	$ _____
_____	_____	Capital:	
		_____	$ _____
Total Assets	$ _____	Total Liabilities and Capital	$ _____

15-H. On the form below, prepare this year's December 31 income statement for a business. Data needed: income from sales, $1,027,800; income from renting equipment to customers, $47,000. Cost of goods sold, $537,400. Expenses include salaries and wages, $145,000; rental of facilities, $170,600; depreciation of equipment, $3,000; electricity, $2,900; supplies, $1,850; and other expenses, $700.

CASWELL AND HOWELL

Revenue:

_____ $ _____

_____ _____

    Total Revenue $ _____

Cost of Goods Sold   _____

Gross Profit $ _____

Operating Expenses:

_____ $ _____

_____ _____

_____ $ _____

_____ _____

_____ $ _____

_____ _____

    Total Operating Expenses   _____

Net Profit (before taxes) $ _____

SMALL GROUP ACTIVITIES

Group Activity 1

Your teacher will put students into groups of two or three. Each group will select or be assigned a different retail store from the community in which to conduct an interview of the manager or person in charge of daily financial operations and cash management. Obtain approval from the store manager for conducting an interview and establish an interview date. Share the purpose of the interview and the type of information needed when arranging for the interview. If possible, ask for a short tour of store operations. Then study the questions listed below and prepare additional questions to ask. Of course, responses from the person you interview may prompt follow-up questions. Make sure to send a thank-you note to the manager following the interview.

1. What qualifications do you require for persons hired into bookkeeping and accounting jobs? Do those employees work in the local store or at a separate location?
2. Does the business use a manual record keeping system, an electronic system, or both?
3. Does the company use a petty cash system? If yes, who is in charge?
4. For what purposes is the petty cash system used?
5. How is the cash used in the business protected against the possibility of theft?
6. What are the requirements for becoming a cashier?
7. What are the established cash register procedures for cashiers when they start and end work each day?
8. What procedure is used to obtain cash needed each day for the registers and to end the day?
9. How much and what kind of training is provided to new employees who must handle money?
10. How has the processing of cash and other customer payments changed in the past several years?

The team should summarize the information obtained from its store and present an oral report to the class. After all teams have reported, a class discussion should be held using the following questions.

1. How do the stores differ on each of the questions asked?
2. In what ways are the stores the same?
3. Did you detect any practices that might not seem adequate to protect the store's cash?
4. What did you learn that was not provided in the text chapter or was different from the textbook?

Group Activity 2

With assistance from your instructor, form a team of three to five students to either (a) work with an existing small business or organization to develop or revise a budget, or (b) form a group interested in budgeting the start of a new business. Possible existing organizations to work with include Boy or Girl Scouts, a civic organization, a church or synagogue, or an organization at your school. Nearly any legal organization that receives and spends money would be appropriate, but obtain approval of your choice from your teacher. Be sure to get information and assistance from the person or group in charge of budgeting and finance in the organization.

Follow the general information in your textbook for creating one of these types of budgets: startup, operating, cash, or capital. The time period could be any length of time up to a year. You may also wish to find other information from your library or the Internet. Place your budget in table format and show what the budget might be under average conditions for an existing business or organization. Show appropriate detail following examples in the chapter.

Once your team has prepared its budget, present it to the class and explain how you arrived at your numbers. Also, discuss the problems the group had in arriving at the projected numbers. What advice would your group give about budget preparation to people planning to start their own businesses?

<table>
<tr><td rowspan="2">Chapter 16

Financing a Business</td><td rowspan="2">Name _____

Date _____</td><td colspan="5" align="center">Scoring Record</td></tr>
<tr><td></td><td>Part A</td><td>Part B</td><td>Part C</td><td>Total</td></tr>
<tr><td></td><td></td><td>Perfect score</td><td>20</td><td>10</td><td>5</td><td>35</td></tr>
<tr><td></td><td></td><td>My score</td><td></td><td></td><td></td><td></td></tr>
</table>

Study Guide

Part A—*Directions:* Indicate your answer to each of the following questions by writing either yes or no in the Answers column.

Answers

1. If you take a partner into your business, is the partner's investment known as creditor capital? .... 1. _____
2. Do businesses in financial difficulty often have trouble getting debt capital? .... 2. _____
3. When others provide equity capital in a sole proprietorship, does the form of business ownership change? .... 3. _____
4. In a partnership, is the money invested by each owner as well as the owners' personal assets at risk if the business fails? .... 4. _____
5. Does common stock represent a type of ownership that gives holders the right to share in the corporation's profits? .... 5. _____
6. When a corporation ceases operations, are preferred and common stockholders likely to get all their investment back from the sale of the assets? .... 6. _____
7. If the par value of a share of stock is $100, can the market value be below $100? .... 7. _____
8. Do current stockholders have the right to buy new issues of stock before they are offered for sale on the open market? .... 8. _____
9. Must corporations keep all retained earnings in the form of cash? .... 9. _____
10. Even when a business is not making a profit, should it plan to replace assets that decrease in value because of obsolescence? .... 10. _____
11. Is a supplier who allows a business 60 days to pay for merchandise providing the business with long-term debt capital? .... 11. _____
12. If a business has an open line of credit, can it borrow an unlimited amount? .... 12. _____
13. Can merchandise inventory be used as security for a loan? .... 13. _____
14. Do sales finance companies buy installment sales contracts from businesses? .... 14. _____
15. Must long-term debt be borrowed for a period of one year or more? .... 15. _____
16. Are unsecured bonds known as debentures? .... 16. _____
17. If a company needs money when interest rates are high, is it better to borrow for a longer period of time? .... 17. _____
18. Do those who provide short-term capital for a business usually have some control over the management of the business? .... 18. _____
19. Does an investment bank make a profit by selling a corporation's bonds to the public for more than it pays to buy the bonds from the corporation? .... 19. _____
20. If stockholders do not want to use their stock options, can they sell their stock rights to others? .... 20. _____

Total Score _____

Part B—*Directions:* For each of the following statements, select the word, or group of words, that best completes the statement. In the Answers column, write the letter corresponding to the answer selected.

1. Money invested in a business by its owner is called (a) retained earnings, (b) working capital, (c) equity capital, (d) creditor capital. .... 1._____

2. Retained earnings refer to (a) profits that owners do NOT save for use by the business, (b) profits that owners do NOT take out of the business, (c) money from the sale of bonds, (d) money from the sale of stock. .... 2._____

3. Preferred stockholders (a) are guaranteed dividends, (b) receive dividends before creditors, (c) typically have voting privileges in a business, (d) receive dividends before common stockholders. .... 3._____

4. Lane owns 50 shares of 7 percent cumulative preferred stock that has a par value of $100 a share. Last year he received no dividends. If profits are large enough this year, in addition to this year's dividends he should receive (a) $35, (b) $350, (c) $500, (d) no additional amount. .... 4._____

5. What usually happens when a corporation ceases operations? (a) Assets that are sold usually raise enough cash to pay the company's debts. (b) Creditors are paid before preferred stockholders are paid. (c) Preferred stockholders are paid before creditors are paid. (d) Common stockholders are paid before creditors are paid. .... 5._____

6. "Plowing back" earnings means (a) distributing all profits earned as dividends to preferred stockholders, (b) distributing all profits earned as dividends to common stockholders, (c) reinvesting some of the profits in the business, (d) distributing all profits earned as dividends to all stockholders. .... 6._____

7. When a business replaces buildings or equipment or adds new facilities for expanding, (a) profits earned cannot be used for these purposes, (b) creditor capital cannot be used for these purposes, (c) profits can be withheld for these purposes, (d) owner capital cannot be used for these purposes. .... 7._____

8. An unconditional promise to pay a lender a certain sum of money at a particular time or on demand is called a (a) promissory note, (b) check, (c) factor, (d) warrant. .... 8._____

9. A contract that allows the use of an asset for a fee is a (a) mortgage, (b) factor, (c) warrant, (d) lease. .... 9._____

10. Which of the following statements is NOT true about bonds? (a) Bonds are long-term debts. (b) The borrowed amount is called the principal. (c) The issuer must pay the bondholder the amount borrowed at the maturity date. (d) Bonds represent a share in the ownership of the corporation. .... 10._____

Total Score _____

Part C—*Directions:* In the Answers column, write the letter of the word or expression in Column I that most closely matches each statement in Column II.

Column I	Column II	Answers
A. bond	1. Ownership that gives holders the right to share in the corporation's profits and to participate in managing the business by voting on basic issues	_____
B. common stock		
C. debentures	2. Permits borrowing up to a specified amount for a specified period of time	_____
D. factor		
E. long-term capital	3. Specializes in lending money to businesses based on their accounts receivable	_____
F. open line of credit		
G. preferred stock	4. A long-term written debt instrument sold by a business to investors, promising to pay a definite sum of money at a specified time	_____
H. venture capital		
	5. Financing obtained from an investor or investment group that lends large sums of money to promising new or expanding small companies	_____
	Total Score	_____

Directions: Study each controversial issue carefully. Follow the advice of your teacher before listing in the columns provided reasons why people might answer Yes or No. Your teacher may want you to work with a class-mate, talk with others in your community to gather information, or use the library or Internet to gather facts.

16-1. Would investing in debenture bonds in a financially strong company be better than investing in mortgage bonds in a financially weak company?

Reasons for "Yes"	Reasons for "No"

16-2. Would stockholders in a strong, growing company prefer to raise additional capital by selling bonds rather than by selling common stock?

Reasons for "Yes"	Reasons for "No"

PROBLEMS

16-A. Use a check mark to indicate whether the sources of capital listed below are equity or debt capital.

Sources of Capital	Equity Capital	Debt Capital
1. Debentures	_____	_____
2. Common stock shares	_____	_____
3. Personal savings invested	_____	_____
4. A short-term loan	_____	_____
5. Preferred stock shares	_____	_____
6. A $5,000 line of credit	_____	_____
7. A mortgage bond for purchase of land ...	_____	_____

16-B. Use the data that follows to answer the questions below: Assets, $2,900,000; Liabilities, $1,400,000; Common Stock (5,000 shares), $1,000,000; Retained Earnings, $500,000; Total Capital, $1,500,000. A share of stock is selling for $225 at stock brokerage houses.

1. What is the book value of a share of stock? $ _____

2. What is the market value of a share of stock? $ _____

3. What is the amount of the equity capital? $ _____

4. Would a bank be willing to loan money to this business?   Yes _____   No _____

   Explain: _____

   _____

5. What is the source of retained earnings? _____

   _____

   _____

16-C. Below is a promissory note. After studying it, answer the questions that follow.

DUE Sept. 15, 20--   NO.   1028

$ 7,500   BALTIMORE, MD., June 15, 20--

Three months ------------ AFTER DATE, WE, OR EITHER OF US, PROMISE TO PAY

TO THE ORDER OF The Bank of Baltimore --------------------------

Seven thousand five hundred xx/100---------------- DOLLARS

WITH ATTORNEY'S FEES. NEGOTIABLE AND PAYABLE AT **INDUSTRIAL TRUST & SAVINGS BANK OF MUNCIE, IND.**, FOR VALUE RECEIVED. WITHOUT RELIEF FROM VALUATION OR APPRAISMENT LAWS. THE DRAWERS AND ENDORSERS SEVERALLY WAIVE PRESENTMENT FOR PAYMENT. PROTEST. NOTICE OF PROTEST AND NOTICE OF NON PAYMENT OF THIS NOTE WITH 10 PERCENT INTEREST AFTER DATE. AND TEN PERCENT INTEREST AFTER MATURITY UNTIL PAID.

John Olivo

Elaine Turk

1. Who owes the money? _____

2. Who is to receive the money when it is due? _____

3. Is this a long-term or a short-term loan? _____

4. For how many months does the business have the use of the borrowed funds? _____

5. Assuming the interest rate is an annual rate, how much interest will the bank receive when the note is due?

   _____

16-D. A corporation issued $150,000 of 8 percent preferred stock and $300,000 of common stock. Profits for the year were $50,000. The board of directors decided to distribute all profits as dividends. Using this data, answer the following questions.

1. How much in dividends will the preferred stockholders receive? _____

2. How much in dividends will the common stockholders receive? _____

3. What percentage return on their investment will preferred stockholders receive? _____

4. What percentage return on their investment will common stockholders receive?

   _____

16-E. Steve Koranski owns a very profitable business. However, he used nearly all his profits by plowing them back into the business. Each year he expanded operations, but cannot quite reach his dream of moving his business into the national market. He has borrowed heavily from banks, and while he has been able to repay his loans, he would like to find a better and less expensive source of funds to grow his business. He recently heard about venture capitalists.

1. Might a venture capitalist be interested in investing a large sum of cash with Steve to expand his business

   nationwide?   Yes _____   No _____

   Why? _____

2. What will a venture capitalist want to know about the business before considering loaning money?

   _____

   _____

   _____

3. What might Steve Koranski have in common with many venture capitalists?

   _____

   _____

   _____

4. What might the venture capitalist want in exchange for the investment?

   _____

   _____

   _____

16-F. The following table shows average bank interest rates on business loans of one year or less for three different years. Using this data, answer the questions that follow.

Size of the Loan	Year #1	Year #2	Year #3
$1,000–$9,999	11.1%	10.1%	10.9%
$10,000–$99,999	11.0	9.9	10.4
$100,000–$499,999	10.7	9.6	9.8
$500,000–$999,999	10.4	9.4	9.5

1. If a business borrowed $15,000 in Year #2, how much would the interest rate have been? _____

2. If a business borrowed $8,000 for all of Year #3, how much interest would it have to pay on the loan?

    _____

3. Is this a long-term or a short-term loan? _____

4. Does it appear that interest rates go up every year?   Yes _____   No _____

5. Does it appear that interest rates go down as loans get larger?   Yes _____   No _____

16-G. Moore Company and Hunt Corporation have 50,000 shares of common stock ($100 par value), which they had both previously sold to stockholders. Each business needs $5 million to expand. Moore Company obtained its $5 million by issuing an additional 50,000 shares of its common stock. Hunt Corporation obtained its $5 million by issuing 5 percent, 20-year bonds with a face value of $5 million. For purposes of this problem, assume the stock and the bonds were sold for enough above par or face value to offset exactly the expenses of selling the stock and bonds.

Both corporations have the same operating profits before paying dividends or bond interest for the next three years, as follows: first year, $500,000; second year, $600,000; third year, $250,000. Assuming that all operating profits were paid out as dividends or bond interest, complete the report below.

	First Year	Second Year	Third Year
Moore Company			
Dividends paid to stockholders	$ _____	$ _____	$ _____
Dividends paid per share	$ _____	$ _____	$ _____
Hunt Corporation			
Interest paid to bondholders	$ _____	$ _____	$ _____
Dividends paid to stockholders	$ _____	$ _____	$ _____
Dividends paid per share	$ _____	$ _____	$ _____

16-H. On July 1, 20--, Acme Corporation issues (sells) $3 million of 8½ percent, 30-year mortgage bonds. The assets pledged as security for the mortgage bond issue include the Acme Corporation's ten-year-old building and five acres of land. Each bond has a face value of $1,000, and the interest is payable semiannually.

1. How many bonds were issued? _____

2. If you owned one of these bonds, how much interest would you receive every six months?

   _____

3. What will be the total amount of interest paid to bondholders during the 30 years?

   _____

4. Must the interest be paid to bondholders before dividends can be paid to the stockholders?

   Yes _____   No _____

5. Does each bondholder possess a share of ownership in Acme Corporation?

   Yes _____   No _____

6. Who holds the mortgage?

   _____

   _____

7. If Acme Corporation failed to pay the interest on the bonds at the end of the sixth year, what might happen?

   _____

   _____

   _____

8. If Acme Corporation should fail, what security do the bondholders have?

   _____

   _____

SMALL GROUP ACTIVITIES

Group Activity 1

Your teacher will place you into groups of three or more students in such a way that there will be an even number of groups. Each group will be numbered, such as one through four. The odd-numbered groups will play the role of entrepreneurs who own a business and need to borrow funds in order to expand. The even-numbered groups will be loan committees from a local bank who make decisions on business financing. Facts about the business borrowers and the banking lenders follow.

The odd-numbered groups (entrepreneurs) own and operate a family-oriented games and sports center that provides batting cages, miniature golf, electronic games, a golf driving range, and go-cart racing. It was the idea of a group of friends who pooled their money and formed a close corporation to start the business. In the three years of its history, it has been reasonably successful. The owners have not had to borrow a substantial amount of money prior to their current need for $200,000. While the business lost money during the first year, it broke even the second year. As it nears the end of its third year, the business is expected to show its first profit, and it has even better financial projections for year four. The majority of the stockholders in this close corporation strongly believe that with borrowed capital, they could open a second store next to a new shopping center being built 20 miles from the original location. One of the stockholders, however, does not believe the new location is all that good and feels it's not time to expand. That stockholder wants to reinvest profits in the original business and add a small restaurant and picnic area.

The even-numbered banking groups will need to decide under what conditions they wish to loan money to the business. Each lending group must decide on the type of financing that is best, and what terms should be offered to this modestly successful corporation. For example, what interest rate should be set in relation to the current average rate for such loans by banks? For how many months should the loan last? What type of collateral, if any, will be required? The lending groups may also raise other questions. The lenders should interview the business owners to gather as much additional information as possible.

The entrepreneur teams will meet to discuss how they can obtain the loan at the lowest rate for a maximum period of time. These groups must also discuss how to answer any questions they might be asked by the lenders. Each lender group needs to come up with a plan that is acceptable to their bank and earns a reasonable profit while minimizing risk. The bank does want to support local businesses when possible. Both teams should investigate types of financing provided to small businesses and the current interest rates for loans.

When both the lending teams and borrowing teams have arrived at a game plan, the two sides must meet, discuss the financing, and arrive at an agreement. Upon completion, the teams should report to the entire class the final borrowing arrangement and also discuss the negotiating styles that each of the teams used in order to arrive at the final agreement.

Group Activity 2

After your teacher has placed you into a group of three to five students, your group is to seek a venture capitalist to help you raise money for your two-year-old Internet company. The company has been rather successful at selling a variety of toys and games online that were popular over 100 years ago. Your company was originally created to gain experience at starting an Internet business. You are proud of what you have learned but are not quite as proud of your results.

You do not know whether the current popularity of your products will continue for very long in the United States. As a result, you want to find old toys and games and perhaps some unique new ones from other countries to expand your market worldwide. To do this, you will need to hire toy and game experts from other countries, enlarge your Web site, establish warehouses, and contract with shipping companies.

You may need as much as $1 million to succeed, and your local lenders are too cautious to loan you money. Thus, you are seeking a venture capitalist who might provide you with at least $500,000 to move ahead with your plan.

At least one of your team members should investigate whether there are other firms who compete with you in your business, online or offline. Your team should also gather as much information as possible about (a) the names and addresses of venture capitalist firms, (b) the kinds of firms they have invested in, (c) the amounts that they typically provide, and (d) the kinds of things they look for before taking a chance with a company like yours. Each member of the team should also search your local area, the library, or the Internet for venture capitalists.

From the evidence that your team members obtain, develop an outline of a financing proposal that a venture capitalist might consider. Then select two actual venture capitalists of those identified who you think would most likely invest in your Internet company. Once this task is done, prepare an introductory letter that might be sent to the venture capitalists together with a proposal that outlines your business experience, expansion plans, and need for funds.

Of course, you will not actually send the letter. Rather, you will share your letter with the class after reporting on the information you gathered, the venture capitalists you found, the two you selected, and other information you feel is important. Other teams will also present their reports. Discuss the results learned after hearing from all teams.

<table>
<tr><td rowspan="3">Chapter 17

Financial Services</td><td rowspan="3">Name _____

Date _____</td><td colspan="4" align="center">Scoring Record</td></tr>
<tr><td></td><td align="center">Part A</td><td align="center">Part B</td><td align="center">Total</td></tr>
<tr><td>Perfect score</td><td align="center">20</td><td align="center">15</td><td align="center">35</td></tr>
<tr><td></td><td>My score</td><td></td><td></td><td></td></tr>
</table>

Study Guide

Part A—*Directions:* Indicate your answer to each of the following questions by writing either yes or no in the Answers column.

Answers

1. Does a bank accept demand deposits as well as make consumer and commercial loans? ... 1. _____
2. Are commercial loans made to individuals as well as to businesses? .... 2. _____
3. Is the primary purpose of nonbank financial institutions to handle demand deposits, commercial loans, and consumer loans? .... 3. _____
4. Do mutual savings banks emphasize long-term loans, such as mortgages, for the local community? .... 4. _____
5. Is the Federal Reserve System (the Fed) the central bank of the United States? .... 5. _____
6. Due to reductions in regulation, do banks and nonbanks offer many of the same products and services today? .... 6. _____
7. Is a promissory note a written order requiring the financial institution to pay previously deposited money to a third party on demand? .... 7. _____
8. With EFT transactions, can money be transferred by computer? .... 8. _____
9. Will the Social Security Administration and the Internal Revenue Service directly deposit checks into customers' bank accounts? .... 9. _____
10. Is a savings bond a negotiable security? .... 10. _____
11. Does a certificate of deposit usually earn a lower interest rate than a savings account? ..... 11. _____
12. Can money market fund depositors withdraw funds by writing checks on the account? 12. _____
13. Does a mutual fund pool the money of many investors primarily for the purchase of stocks and bonds? .... 13. _____
14. Are treasury instruments short- and long-term securities sold to finance the cost of running the government?.. 14. _____
15. Is a treasury bond the longest-term government security? .... 15. _____
16. Does a CD have greater liquidity than a checking account? .... 16. _____
17. Do investors diversify to reduce risk?.. 17. _____
18. Are investors who buy stock in newly developed corporations looking for maximum security? .... 18. _____
19. Is NASDAQ the nation's first electronic stock market? .... 19. _____
20. Can most skilled investors usually predict when the market will reach its high and low points? .... 20. _____

Total Score   _____

Part B—*Directions:* For each of the following statements, select the word, or group of words, that best completes the statement. In the Answers column, write the letter corresponding to the answer selected.

1. Which service is NOT typically provided by commercial banks? (a) offer financial and tax advice, (b) provide bill-paying and payroll preparation services, (c) collect promissory notes and sell insurance, (d) sell treasury notes and treasury bonds. ....   1. _____

2. Not-for-profit financial institutions owned by their members are known as (a) commercial banks, (b) credit unions, (c) savings and loan associations, (d) mutual insurance companies.   2. _____

3. All of the following are nonbank institutions EXCEPT (a) stock brokerage firms, (b) savings and loan associations, (c) insurance companies, (d) finance companies. ....   3. _____

4. The endorsement "For Deposit Only, Big Blue Corporation" is known as a (a) blank endorsement, (b) full endorsement, (c) restrictive endorsement, (d) special endorsement. ....   4. _____

5. When you endorse a check, you should use a full endorsement when you want to (a) limit the use of the funds in some way, (b) transfer the rights to the funds to someone else, (c) allow anyone to cash the check, (d) deposit the funds. ....   5. _____

6. An unsecured loan is one that is not backed by (a) the U.S. government, (b) a profitable business, (c) collateral, (d) a written promise to pay. ....   6. _____

7. The lowest rate of interest at which large banks lend large sums to the best-qualified borrowers is the (a) prime rate, (b) industry rate, (c) secured rate, (d) consumer rate. ....   7. _____

8. Which transaction CANNOT be handled by EFT? (a) Internet banking, (b) direct deposits, (c) payroll preparation, (d) debit-card payments. ....   8. _____

9. With ATMs, bank customers can make (a) deposits but not withdrawals, (b) withdrawals but not deposits, (c) deposits and withdrawals and transfer funds, (d) deposits and withdrawals but cannot transfer funds. ....   9. _____

10. If your bank's ATM fee is $7.50 to withdraw $500.00 and you withdraw the money from a competitor's ATM that charges $9.00, by how much would your bank account be reduced? (a) $483.50, (b) $507.50, (c) $509.00, (d) $516.50. ....   10. _____

11. Which statement is INCORRECT about CDs? (a) CDs can be purchased for periods ranging from three months to five years. (b) CDs can be purchased for any amount with no minimum. (c) Checking accounts usually pay a lower rate of interest than do CDs. (d) Interest rates vary in relation to the term of the CD. ....   11. _____

12. The use of money to make more money is know as (a) a loan, (b) an investment, (c) profit, (d) collateral. ....   12. _____

13. Which factor should NOT be considered when setting investment goals? (a) liquidity, (b) safety, (c) growth, (d) reputation. ....   13. _____

14. Corporations that want to sell their stock to investors must be listed on (a) a stock exchange (b) a securities listing, (c) an electronic trading board, (d) an EFT. ....   14. _____

15. Which of the following is NOT the name of a stock index? (a) NASDAQ Market Index, (b) Dow Jones Industrial Average, (c) Commodities Exchange Index, (d) Standard & Poor's 500. ....   15. _____

Total Score   _____

Name _____

Directions: Study each controversial issue carefully. Follow the advice of your teacher before listing in the columns provided reasons why people might answer Yes or No. Your teacher may want you to work with a classmate, talk with others in your community to gather information, or use the library or Internet to gather facts.

17-1. Because most financial institutions provide similar services, should we stop using specific names like savings and loan associations, credit unions, mutual savings banks, and financial services companies and let any business that offers a variety of financial services use the name "bank"?

Reasons for "Yes"	Reasons for "No"

17-2. Because of the growing security risks and amount of identity theft, should the use of EFT and other online financial services be highly regulated and restricted?

Reasons for "Yes"	Reasons for "No"

PROBLEMS

17-A. Check whether the following financial institutions would be classified as a bank or a nonbank.

Type of Financial Institution	Bank	Nonbank
1. Financial services company	_____	_____
2. Mutual fund	_____	_____
3. Savings and loan association	_____	_____
4. Commercial bank	_____	_____
5. Credit union	_____	_____
6. Federal Reserve System (Fed)	_____	_____

17-B. Because computers are used extensively in banking, many EFT services are available. For each service below, list two advantages. List any disadvantages of using the electronic services.

1. Direct Deposit

   Advantages: _____

   _____

   _____

   _____

   Disadvantages: _____

   _____

   _____

   _____

2. ATM

   Advantages: _____

   _____

   _____

   _____

   Disadvantages: _____

   _____

   _____

   _____

3. Online banking

Advantages: _____

_____

_____

_____

Disadvantages: _____

_____

_____

_____

17-C. Check the appropriate column for the maturity date for each financial instrument purchased for its shortest life.

Financial Instrument	No Maturity Date	One Year or Less	One Year or More
1. Treasury bill	_____	_____	_____
2. Certificate of deposit	_____	_____	_____
3. Savings account	_____	_____	_____
4. Treasury note	_____	_____	_____
5. Treasury bond	_____	_____	_____
6. Mutual fund	_____	_____	_____
7. Money market account	_____	_____	_____

17-D. For each investment goal shown in the columns on the right, place a check mark in the column that would most likely represent the investment goal for each situation described.

	Liquidity	Safety	Growth
1. Juan is 35, single, and a lawyer in a corporation.	_____	_____	_____
2. Martin is 22, single, and just started a new business.	_____	_____	_____
3. Jackie is 60, single, and has a nice retirement fund built up. ...	_____	_____	_____
4. Wanda is 67 and wants to help her young grandchildren with college expenses.	_____	_____	_____
5. Jim and Laura are 48, have two teens, and own a very profitable business.	_____	_____	_____
6. Terry is 39, newly married, and just lost his job due to downsizing.	_____	_____	_____

17-E. Below are three different types of mutual funds. Four individuals recently invested $5,000 each on the same day, divided among the different funds as shown. Their choice of investments strongly suggests their investment goals. First, calculate the percentage that each person invested in each fund. Then answer the questions that follow.

	Growth Fund	%	Mony Market Fund	%	Bond Fund	%
Crowley	0	_____	$3,500	_____	$1,500	_____
Galvin	$4,000	_____	0	_____	$1,000	_____
Harriman	$2,500	_____	0	_____	$2,500	_____
Amanai	$1,000	_____	$500	_____	$3,500	_____

1. What appears to be Crowley's primary investment goal or goals? _____

_____

2. What appears to be Galvin's primary investment goal or goals? _____

_____

3. What appears to be Harriman's primary investment goal or goals? _____

_____

4. What appears to be Amani's primary investment goal or goals? _____

_____

5. How would you invest the $5,000 to represent your investment goals? _____

_____

17-F. A business needs checks written and endorsed. Assume you are the accountant for the business. Complete the tasks specified for each check below. Use correct procedures.

1. Write the following check to Harrison Brothers for $925.50.

The Collision Shop		1205
425 Munson Avenue		
Los Angeles, CA 90910	_____ 20 _____	72-2029/290

PAY TO THE
ORDER OF _____ $ _____

_____ DOLLARS

FOR CLASSROOM USE ONLY

THE FIRST NATIONAL BANK
ANYWHERE, CA 90343

MEMO _____   _____

|:27629290|:   1205

2. Write the following check to Karen Anderson for $110.

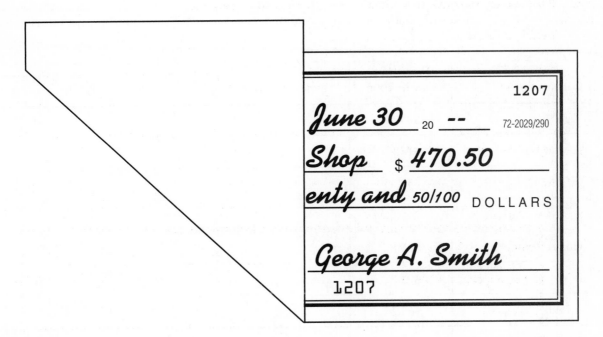

The Collision Shop
425 Munson Avenue
Los Angeles, CA 90910

1206

_____ 20 _____   72-2029/290

PAY TO THE
ORDER OF _____ $ _____

_____ DOLLARS

FOR CLASSROOM USE ONLY

THE FIRST NATIONAL BANK
ANYWHERE, CA 90343

MEMO _____   _____

|:27629290|:   1206

3. Endorse the following check that will later be mailed to your bank for deposit in your business checking account.

1207

June 30 20 `--`   72-2029/290

Shop $ *470.50* _____

enty and 50/100 DOLLARS

George A. Smith _____

1207

4. Endorse the following check that you are transferring to Maxine Wexton.

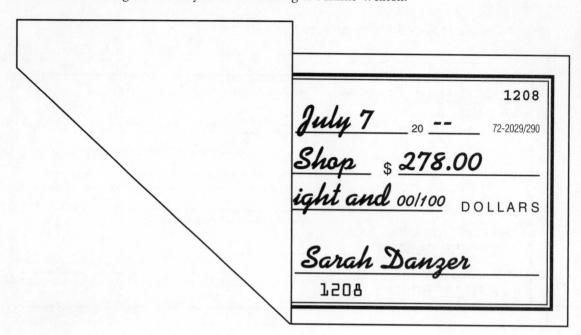

July 7 _____ 20 -- _____ 72-2029/290

Shop _____ $ 278.00 _____

ight and 00/100 DOLLARS

Sarah Danzer

1208

1208

17-G. Below is a list of major American corporations and the cost per share of stock on a particular day in the year 2006. For each of the next three days, find the price of each stock by checking the New York Stock Exchange section of a newspaper or the Internet. In the columns below, record the date and share price for each day. From the stock listings, select the price shown in the columns labeled "last" for the common stock, not preferred (pfd) stock. Then answer the questions below. (If you cannot find a stock listed, check to see if the company has changed its name, merged with another firm, gone bankrupt, been purchased by another firm, or transferred to another stock exchange.)

Corporation	Price on a Day in 2006	Date	Price	Date	Price	Date	Price
Wal-Mart	$45.58						
Ford Motor	$18.26						
Citigroup	$50.41						
Southwest Airlines	$15.62						
Home Depot	$38.82						
IBM	$91.22						
Allstate	$63.12						
Coca-Cola	$46.41						
OfficeMax	$46.59						
Kellogg's	$49.71						

1. Which three stocks show the best overall gain since the year 2006?

   _____

2. Which three stocks show the least gain, or the greatest loss, since the year 2006?

   _____

3. In which one company would you invest money if you were 25 years of age? If you were 60 years of age?

   _____

   _____

4. If someone owned one share in each of the companies on that day in 2006, what would be the person's total value of all stocks? What would the average price per share have been?

   _____

5. If someone owned one share of stock in each of the companies on your third day, what is the total value of the stocks owned? What is the average price per share?

   _____

6. Using your answers for questions 4 and 5, what would be the total and per-share gain or loss in dollars and as a percentage for those time periods?

   _____

SMALL GROUP ACTIVITIES

Group Activity 1

In teams of three people each, identify a local commercial bank, savings bank, savings and loan association, and nonbank financial institution. Obtain a list of the main financial products and services offered to customers as well as the fees that are charged for the services. Summarize the services and fees of the four local financial institutions and analyze the information.

Second, find three financial institutions on the Internet that provide a range of financial services including checking accounts, savings accounts, and loans, including home mortgages. Obtain the fees that are charged for the services. Summarize the services and rates and analyze the information.

Third, compare the services and fees between the local brick-and-mortar financial institutions and those found on the Internet. Summarize the similarities and differences of services and interest rates and costs of services. Identify the most significant differences between various types of financial institutions and between local and online institutions. Provide an opinion from your team under what circumstances a local walk-in financial institution is better and under what conditions an online financial institution is better. Be sure to identify the advantages and disadvantages of each. You may be asked to present a brief oral report to the class or a written report to your teacher. Follow the instructions of your teacher for how to present your final report.

Group Activity 2

Many businesses and individuals simplify their investments by dealing with just one mutual fund company that offers many types of funds, such as money market accounts, bond funds, growth funds, and international funds. A mutual fund's family of funds permits investors to invest money in one or many funds to meet their investment goals.

Your teacher will divide the class into groups of three to five members. Your group is a new financial consulting firm. One of your customers is a small successful firm that wants to invest $190,000. The company's CEO told you that $45,000 must always be readily available during the year but should earn a good interest rate. You will be given about a three-month notice before those funds will be needed. Half of the remaining funds should be in somewhat safe investments while the remaining funds can be invested for growth purposes. Those funds do not need to be particularly liquid. Up to 15 percent of the funds can be used for more risky investments as long as the rate of return is expected to be high.

Your team is to select one mutual fund company from among the many that are available in which you can invest your customer's funds. *Caution:* Some mutual fund companies subtract a percentage of the amount to be invested as their service fee, while others do not. This fee may upset your customer. After you have selected a family of mutual funds, prepare a plan for investing the $190,000. When done, you should show the specific fund names, brief information about the past success of each fund, the amount to be invested in each fund, and an explanation of why you picked each fund to meet specific objectives.

Fund information is available from many sources, including libraries, Internet sites, and stock brokerage firms. In particular, seek the ratings of funds from an organization called Morningstar that is available at stock brokerage firms and online (www.morningstar.com).

Prepare your information and present it as an oral or written report to your customer, as specified by your teacher. Your teacher, and possibly your class, will review your report and decide whether to accept it or ask you to improve it.

<table>
<tr><td rowspan="2">Chapter 18

Credit and Insurance</td><td rowspan="2">Name _____

Date _____</td><td colspan="5" align="center">Scoring Record</td></tr>
<tr><td></td><td>Part A</td><td>Part B</td><td>Part C</td><td>Total</td></tr>
</table>

		Part A	Part B	Part C	Total
	Perfect score	20	10	5	35
	My score				

Study Guide

Part A—*Directions:* Indicate your answer to each of the following questions by writing either yes or no in the Answers column.

Answers

1. Must businesses that want to sell on credit work with one or more of the major credit card companies? .... 1. _____

2. Is a merchant account provider a private company that acts as an intermediary between businesses and one or more credit card companies? .... 2. _____

3. Do some businesses still process credit card transactions without using a computerized credit card system? .... 3. _____

4. Are the terms and fees of most credit card company and bank agreements the same? .... 4. _____

5. Is the most popular form of installment credit known as revolving credit? .... 5. _____

6. Are Visa and MasterCard examples of nonbank credit cards? .... 6. _____

7. Does a debit card immediately transfer funds electronically from the customer's checking account to the business's account when a purchase is made? .... 7. _____

8. Is a smart card just another name for a debit card? .... 8. _____

9. Are character, capacity, capital, and credit the four Cs for determining creditworthiness? 9. _____

10. Is Dun & Bradstreet, Inc. an important source of information on the credit standing of retailers, wholesalers, and manufacturers? .... 10. _____

11. Are the two major objectives of a collection procedure to collect the amount due and to retain the goodwill of the customer? .... 11. _____

12. Does a firm's cash flow increase when its bad debts increase? .... 12. _____

13. Is insurance most often purchased when a company faces the risk of nonfinancial losses? 13. _____

14. Should a business be able to predict whether it will have specific losses and the amount of those losses during the year? .... 14. _____

15. Is a risk defined as the uncertainty that a loss may occur? .... 15. _____

16. Are insurance companies required by law to charge the same rates for a certain amount of insurance no matter what the level of risk? .... 16. _____

17. Must the policyholder have an insurable interest in the property in order to purchase insurance? .... 17. _____

18. When purchasing insurance, should the purchaser be concerned about the insurance company's reputation for paying claims in the event of a loss? .... 18. _____

19. Does transportation insurance protect people if they are injured while traveling by air, automobile, or bus? .... 19. _____

20. Are changes in fashion and styles considered noninsurable risks? .... 20. _____

Total Score   _____

Part B—*Directions:* For each of the following statements, select the word, or group of words, that best completes the statement. In the Answers column, write the letter corresponding to the answer selected.

1. An example of installment credit is a (a) manufacturer giving a retailer thirty days to pay for merchandise, (b) bank providing a business loan, (c) customer purchasing an automobile and agreeing to make monthly payments over a five-year period, (d) retailer holding a purchase until the last payment is made. .... 1. _____

2. An advantage of a debit card for a bank is that (a) the bank doesn't have to send a transaction statement to its customers, (b) the bank doesn't have to bill and collect from customers, (c) the bank doesn't have to charge interest, (d) the bank doesn't have to charge a service fee. 2. _____

3. What is the best single measure of whether to grant credit to an applicant? (a) Type of job held by the applicant. (b) Length of time applicant has held the job. (c) Total debts owed by the applicant. (d) Past credit-paying record of the applicant. .... 3. _____

4. Under the Fair Credit Reporting Act, people (a) have the right to see their credit agency reports but do not have the right to have errors corrected, (b) have the right to see their credit agency reports and have errors corrected, (c) have the right to know why their credit application was rejected, (d) have the right to see their credit reports before credit agencies file them. 4. _____

5. If the amount of accounts receivable for a business steadily increased over the last six months, but its credit sales remained about the same, bad debt losses are likely to (a) gradually disappear, (b) stay about the same, (c) increase, (d) decrease. .... 5. _____

6. To pay claims, insurance companies use money collected from (a) the federal government, (b) the insured, (c) policyholders, (d) losses. .... 6. _____

7. Most insurance contracts are purchased from (a) policyholders, (b) banks, (c) insurance actuaries, (d) insurance agents. .... 7. _____

8. Organizations that provide an alternative to traditional health insurance include all of the following EXCEPT (a) health and wellness centers, (b) preferred provider organizations (PPOs), (c) health maintenance organizations (HMOs), (d) all of the responses are correct. 8. _____

9. Typical business insurance policies usually do NOT cover losses resulting from (a) burglaries and robberies, (b) international business operations, (c) the death of an executive, (d) injury to customers caused by the business's product. .... 9. _____

10. Which of the following procedures should businesses consider using to protect important documents and records? (a) Make duplicate copies of all records. (b) Store copies in a separate location from originals. (c) Prepare and practice a disaster plan. (d) All of the procedures should be followed. .... 10. _____

Total Score   _____

Part C—*Directions:* In the Answers column, write the letter of the word or expression in Column I that most closely matches each statement in Column II.

Column I	Column II	Answers
A. Equal Credit Opportunity Act	1. Gives women the same credit rights as men	_____
B. insurance	2. A payment to the insurer for protection against a risk	_____
C. Truth-in-Lending Law	3. Requires businesses to reveal the total cost of credit and finance charges on credit forms and statements	_____
D. actuaries	4. Protects people from abusive, deceptive, and unfair practices from debt collectors	_____
E. Fair Debt Collection Practices Act	5. Responsible for calculating the rates insurance companies must charge to cover losses and make a profit	_____
F. premium		

Total Score   _____

Directions: Study each controversial issue carefully. Follow the advice of your teacher before listing in the columns provided reasons why people might answer Yes or No. Your teacher may want you to work with a class-mate, talk with others in your community to gather information, or use the library or Internet to gather facts.

18-1. Consumers have the right to review their credit records under the Fair Credit Reporting Act, even though few do until a problem arises. Consequently, should credit reporting agencies be required to mail to consumers a copy of all information in their credit file every few years, even if the customer hasn't requested a copy?

Reasons for "Yes"	Reasons for "No"

18-2. In many states, insurance companies are allowed to cancel property and liability insurance contracts if they believe the risk has increased. This means that people who have had an expensive claim on their auto insurance or have received a couple of tickets while driving may have their insurance cancelled. Should states pass laws to require insurance companies to continue to offer automobile insurance to people who are willing and able to pay their premiums, even if the level of risk has increased?

Reasons for "Yes"	Reasons for "No"

PROBLEMS

18-A. For each of the descriptions below, select the type of financial transaction card being described and write it in the blank space provided. The choices of card types are smart card, affinity card, store credit card, debit card, and co-branded card.

Description	Type of Card
1. A shopper uses her Home Depot card to buy paint and painting supplies.	_____
2. A graduate of Stanford University uses his MasterCard with the university's logo to support the alumni association...	_____
3. Delta Air Lines runs a special promotion for customers who use the Delta SkyMiles American Express card to purchase tickets....................................	_____
4. When purchasing groceries at a supermarket, a customer checks his checking account balance before swiping his card................................	_____
5. When visiting his doctor, a patient gives his plastic card to the receptionist to be scanned for updated personal information.	_____

18-B. Joel Bender has applied for credit to buy a car on the installment plan. He possesses certain characteristics that might affect his request for credit.

1. Classify each characteristic on the form below.

	Character	Capacity	Capital	Conditions
a. Has a steady, high-paying job.	____	____	____	____
b. Does not have much money in his bank accounts. Keeps his checking account balance very low.	____	____	____	____
c. Has purchased a nice home but has a large mortgage..	____	____	____	____
d. Has a poor credit record. Frequently pays bills late and has never paid a few small bills.............	____	____	____	____
e. Has lost several jobs because of excessive absenteeism.	____	____	____	____
f. A recession is affecting his employer's business. ..	____	____	____	____

2. Is Joel Bender a good candidate for obtaining the credit he desires?   Yes _____   No _____

Reasons for your answer: _____

_____

_____

18-C. The annual sales and the loss on bad debts in each of five business firms are given below. For each firm, determine what percent of the sales is represented by the loss on bad debts.

Business	Sales	Loss on Bad Debts	Percent
Hart Company	$300,000	$ 3,000	_____
Cable & Cable	200,000	1,000	_____
Bell Corporation	400,000	3,600	_____
Wahl Appliances	500,000	7,500	_____
Eastern Corporation	600,000	12,000	_____

18-D. On the next page is a credit application form. Use the following information to complete the form. Leave blank any item for which information is not provided.

The applicant is Arnold Prince, age 41, who lives at 15 Oak Lane, Atlanta, GA 30315-5391. His home telephone number is 404-555-6842, and his social security number is 057-28-8375. Mr. Prince is married, has two children, and has owned his own home for five years. His monthly mortgage payment is $1,250.

The applicant has worked for Cabinets, Inc. (2183 Pine St., Atlanta, GA) as a carpenter and earns an average of $52,000 a year. The company makes kitchen cabinets that are sold to contractors. The business phone number is 404-555-5921. Prior to obtaining his job five years ago, Mr. Prince worked for the Long Lumber Co. in Atlanta on Worth Avenue. He was with the company for two years.

Arnold Prince's wife, Marilyn, age 38, is not currently working for an employer. Her social security number is 061-21-7451.

The Princes have their checking and savings accounts at the same bank: First National Bank, Main Street, Atlanta. The checking account number is 57918, and the money market account number is 57-302. They have a charge account, No. B-78-3564, at Wiley's Department Store with a $115 balance. They buy all their gas for the family car using a Stahl credit card, No. 214-35-892, which they just paid in full. The Princes are requesting $2,500 of credit and would like two credit cards. Sign for Marilyn and Arnold Prince using today's date.

18-E. Your credit manager handed you the report below. Study it and answer the following questions.

Comparative Analysis of Past-Due Accounts

Days Past Due	Current Month	Percent	Prior Month	Percent	Increase (Decrease)
1–30	$ 2,580,300	_____	$ 1,335,000	_____	$ _____
31–60	393,800	_____	171,200	_____	_____
61–90	330,700	_____	346,100	_____	_____
Over 90	94,500	_____	49,500	_____	_____
Totals	$ _____	100.0%	$ _____	100.0%	$ _____

1. Complete the report.

2. By what percent did past-due accounts increase over last month? _____

3. Should the credit manager be concerned?   Yes _____   No _____

   Explain: _____

   _____

   _____

4. What are two possible reasons for the changes that have occurred?

   _____

   _____

Kramer's Application for Credit

☐ **Individual Account**—Complete sections A, B, C, E. You may designate one authorized user, for whose payments you will be responsible, by writing only his/her name and relationship in section D.

☐ **Joint Account**—Complete sections A through E.

Section A—Tell us about yourself

LAST NAME	FIRST NAME	MIDDLE		SOCIAL SECURITY NO.	AGE

HOME ADDRESS	CITY	STATE	ZIP CODE	HOME PHONE ( )	NO. OF DEPENDENTS

☐ OWN ☐ ROOM & BOARD ☐ LIVE WITH PARENTS ☐ RENT FURNISHED ☐ RENT UNFURNISHED ☐ MOBILE HOME ☐ OTHER	TIME AT THIS ADDRESS YRS. MOS.	MONTHLY RENT/MORTGAGE $

PREVIOUS HOME ADDRESS (IF LESS THAN 3 YEARS AT PRESENT ADDRESS)	TIME AT PREVIOUS ADDRESS YRS. MOS.

NAME AND ADDRESS OF NEAREST RELATIVE NOT LIVING WITH APPLICANT	RELATIVE HOME PHONE ( )

Section B—Tell us about your employment

BUSINESS OR EMPLOYER	TYPE OF BUSINESS	BUSINESS PHONE ( )	EXT.

BUSINESS ADDRESS	CITY	STATE	ZIP CODE	EDUCATION ☐ GRADUATE ☐ COLLEGE ☐ HIGH SCHOOL ☐ ELEMENTARY

POSITION OR TITLE	HOW LONG WITH THIS EMPLOYER? YRS. MOS.	ANNUAL SALARY $

PREVIOUS BUSINESS/EMPLOYER (IF LESS THAN 3 YEARS AT THIS JOB)	HOW LONG? YRS. MOS.	POSITION OR TITLE

OTHER INCOME: ALIMONY, CHILD SUPPORT, OR SEPARATE MAINTENANCE INCOME NEED NOT BE REVEALED IF YOU DO NOT WISH TO HAVE IT CONSIDERED AS A BASIS FOR REPAYING THIS OBLIGATION.	ANNUAL AMOUNT $	SOURCE

Section C—Tell us about your credit and banking relationships

BANK REFERENCES—NAMES OF BANKS AND BRANCH LOCATIONS	ACCOUNT NUMBERS	BALANCE
1.		$
2.		$

CREDIT REFERENCES—ACCOUNTS WITH DEPT. STORES, BANK CARDS, OIL COMPANIES	ACCOUNT NUMBERS	BALANCE
1.		$
2.		$

OUTSTANDING LOANS (NAME OF CREDITOR/CREDIT UNION/FINANCE COMPANY)

OTHER CREDIT REFERENCES	HAVE YOU EVER HAD ANOTHER KRAMER'S ACCOUNT?	ACCOUNT NO. (IF KNOWN)

Section D—Information regarding joint applicant or authorized user

LAST NAME	FIRST NAME	MIDDLE		SOCIAL SECURITY NO.	AGE

BUSINESS OR EMPLOYER	TYPE OF BUSINESS	BUSINESS PHONE ( )	EXT.

BUSINESS ADDRESS	CITY	STATE	ZIP CODE	EDUCATION ☐ GRADUATE ☐ COLLEGE ☐ HIGH SCHOOL ☐ ELEMENTARY

POSITION OR TITLE	HOW LONG WITH THIS EMPLOYER? YRS. MOS.	ANNUAL SALARY $

RELATIONSHIP TO APPLICANT	OTHER INCOME: ALIMONY, CHILD SUPPORT, OR SEPARATE MAINTENANCE INCOME NEED NOT BE REVEALED IF YOU DO NOT WISH TO HAVE IT CONSIDERED AS A BASIS FOR REPAYING THIS OBLIGATION.	ANNUAL AMOUNT $	SOURCE

Section E—Optional Accountguard Credit Insurance Plan

Please enroll me in the Accountguard Credit Insurance Plan providing the coverages described and at the cost set forth on the reverse. I understand it is not required to obtain credit and will not be provided unless I sign below and pay the additional cost disclosed on the reverse.

☐ YES _____, I want ____/____/____ 　　☐ NO _____, I do not want Accountguard Credit Insurance
　　　　　initial　　　　birthdate　　　　　　　　　　initial

Section F—Please sign here and on reverse side

I (We) understand that you may investigate my (our) credit record and may report information concerning the credit experience of the Account for individual and joint accountholders and authorized users to consumer reporting agencies and others.

If Applicant signs on behalf of Joint Applicant, Applicant represents that he or she is authorized to make this application.

I (We) agree to terms of the **RETAIL INSTALLMENT CREDIT AGREEMENT** on reverse side.

X _____
APPLICANT'S SIGNATURE　　　　　　　DATE

X _____
JOINT APPLICANT'S SIGNATURE　　　　DATE

Name _____

18-F. The Autocity Taxi Company owns and operates a fleet of 100 taxis. It pays an annual insurance premium of $960 per taxi. Thirty percent of the premium pays for liability and medical payments coverage while 70 percent provides collision and comprehensive coverage. During the past five years, Autocity has had the following record of losses covered by collision and comprehensive insurance:

Year 1 $75,000
Year 2 $52,000
Year 3 $43,000
Year 4 $68,000
Year 5 $74,000

Autocity is considering dropping its coverage for collision and comprehensive and putting the money it saves into an account to pay for damage to its taxis.

1. If Autocity had followed its plan for the past five years, how much money could have been saved?

_____

_____

_____

2. What other factors should Autocity consider before deciding to drop the insurance coverage?

_____

_____

_____

_____

_____

_____

18-G. The Monumental Insurance Company sells life insurance. Premiums for each $1,000 of ordinary life insurance are shown in the following table. The smallest policy the company sells is for $5,000 coverage. Premiums may be paid once a year (annually), twice a year (semiannually), or four times a year (quarterly). Study the table and answer the questions that follow.

Age Nearest Birthday	Premiums		
	Annually	Semiannually	Quarterly
25	$10.13	$5.27	$2.74
26	$10.50	$5.46	$2.84
27	$10.86	$5.65	$2.93
28	$11.26	$5.86	$3.04
29	$11.68	$6.07	$3.15
30	$12.07	$6.28	$3.26
31	$12.47	$6.48	$3.37
32	$12.90	$6.71	$3.48
33	$13.34	$6.94	$3.60
34	$13.81	$7.18	$3.73
35	$14.30	$7.44	$3.86

1. What is the quarterly premium for Beth Williams? She purchased a $50,000 policy at age 34.

   _____

2. What is the semiannual premium for John VanDyke? He purchased a $20,000 policy at age 25.

   _____

3. What is the annual premium for Earl McCauley? He purchased a $35,000 policy at age 28.

   _____

4. What is the yearly premium for Alice Evans. She purchased a $15,000 policy at age 30, but pays premiums quarterly. _____

5. If Alice Evans paid premiums annually rather than quarterly, how much would she save yearly?

   _____

6. Give a reason why total premiums are less if paid once a year than premiums paid four times a year.

   _____

   _____

18-H. Identify the following risks as normally being insurable or noninsurable by placing a check mark in the appropriate column.

Description of Risk	Insurable	Noninsurable
1. Due to a cold and rainy summer season, a clothing store, unable to sell much of its inventory of swimwear, cannot pay the supplier.	_____	_____
2. Because of improper storage procedures, a manufacturer finds that a large quantity of the raw materials used in production has been damaged and cannot be used.	_____	_____
3. A trucking company has had a very large contract with a wholesaler for the past five years. During the last six months, several of the older trucks have had an unusual number of breakdowns resulting in problems delivering the wholesaler's orders. As a result, the wholesaler has refused to sign a new contract with the trucking company.	_____	_____
4. An insurance company has computer records of all policies and stores them in a vault in another city to protect against loss in case of fire or other damage to its headquarters building. However, the company would still face a significant expense if the original records were destroyed.	_____	_____
5. A company had just purchased several new vehicles that were parked on the street waiting to be serviced before the company's salespeople picked them up. During the night, an uninsured driver lost control of his car while driving by the vehicles. Three of the vehicles had major damage while two others had minor damage.	_____	_____

SMALL GROUP ACTIVITIES

Group Activity 1

Your teacher will divide the class into three to five teams. Each team is to obtain a list of commercial banks in your geographic area, then select several preferred banks to contact. However, before contacting any bank, the team leaders should meet and agree on which banks each team will contact so that no bank is contacted by more than one team. Your team will identify and make arrangements for meeting with a bank representative. A meeting time and date should be established early.

Your main topic is: What are the procedures, policies, and problems that arise when a new business sets up and operates a credit card system that involves a national credit card company such as Visa or MasterCard? You will want your banker to explain and show how a credit card account system is established and maintained for small businesses. Prior to the meeting, the team must meet to prepare and discuss a set of key questions that you will ask on the topic. For example, you may wish to know the specific kinds of problems that most often occur with new businesses regarding credit card accounts. Your banker may wish to see the questions in advance.

Work out the meeting date and time with the banker. The banker may prefer that you go to the bank where you can be shown forms, policies, electronic equipment, and procedures that the bank uses in working with business credit card accounts. Helpful brochures may also be available.

After your visit, prepare a report to share with the class. Summarize the most important points learned. Other teams will also present their reports. Comparisons among the teams will allow you to better understand the importance of banks to everyone and how banks might have different approaches to achieving their goals of serving entrepreneurs. When finished, prepare a special note of thanks and give it to your teacher to review. Then send it to the banker.

Group Activity 2

Risks pose important concerns to businesspeople. The business that does an effective job of managing risks has a better chance of being successful than those that do not manage risks effectively. For this activity, your class needs to be divided into teams of three or four students. Each team will review business magazines, newspapers, and Internet sites that provide general business information. Each team should collect as many examples as possible of reports of risks that businesses have faced. Write a two- or three-sentence description of each example on a note card.

When the examples have been collected, each team should prepare a poster with the following headings across the top of the poster—Insurable, Noninsurable—and the following listed on the left side of the poster—Managed Successfully, Managed Unsuccessfully. The result will be four categories on the poster. Now, as a team, decide into which category each note card should be placed and write the category name on the back of the card.

Each team, in turn, should read the information on their note cards to the other teams. The first team to identify the correct category receives a point. (In case of a disagreement, your teacher will identify the correct category.) After all teams have read their note cards, tally the team points and identify the team with the most points.

As a final activity, look at the examples categorized as "Managed Unsuccessfully." The entire class should discuss the risks described and decide how the business could have responded better to each of the risks.

Chapter 19		Scoring Record				
Product Planning and Production Management	Name _____ Date _____		**Part A**	**Part B**	**Part C**	**Total**
		Perfect score	20	10	5	35
		My score				

Study Guide

Part A—*Directions:* Indicate your answer to each of the following questions by writing either yes or no in the Answers column.

Answers

1. Is it possible for companies to spend several million dollars to develop and manufacture one new product? .... 1. _____

2. Do nearly 90 percent of new products developed by businesses survive in the market for at least five years? .... 2. _____

3. Are most of the products you will be using in 10 years currently for sale on the market? 3. _____

4. For a company to survive, must it continually search for ways to improve even its most successful products? .... 4. _____

5. Should companies rely on scientists and engineers for their new product ideas? .... 5. _____

6. Are customers reliable sources of product development information? .... 6. _____

7. Is research that is done without a specific product in mind known as pure research? .... 7. _____

8. Should research and testing on new products be conducted before the product is produced and marketed? .... 8. _____

9. Is manufacturing a form of production that turns raw and semifinished materials into finished products? .... 9. _____

10. Does manufacturing require the use of assembly lines and mass production? .... 10. _____

11. Is the conversion of iron ore into steel an example of continuous processing? .... 11. _____

12. Has the assembly line concept changed significantly since Henry Ford used the idea to produce cars? .... 12. _____

13. Should a company that uses a large quantity of raw materials attempt to locate close to the source of those materials? .... 13. _____

14. Is customer location an important factor to consider when deciding where to locate a new production facility? .... 14. _____

15. Do some cities offer reduced tax rates or even remove some taxes in order to encourage new businesses to locate there? .... 15. _____

16. Are the three important production planning activities inventory management, human resource planning, and production scheduling? .... 16. _____

17. Did U.S. businesses initially ignore Dr. W. Edward Deming's ideas on quality management? 17. _____

18. Do robots now complete just the most complex and difficult production processes? .... 18. _____

19. Have service businesses grown at a slower rate than manufacturing businesses? .... 19. _____

20. Does the quality of a service usually depend on who provides the service? .... 20. _____

Total Score _____

Part B—*Directions:* For each of the following statements, select the word, or group of words, that best completes the statement. In the Answers column, write the letter corresponding to the answer selected.

1. The process of creating or improving a product is known as (a) marketing, (b) pure research, (c) logistics, (d) product development. .... 1. _____

2. A consumer panel is made up of people who (a) do not know the company, (b) have worked for the competitor, (c) sell products to the company's customers, (d) have bought or are likely to buy the company's products. .... 2. _____

3. Substituting plastics for metal parts in an automobile to reduce weight and improve efficiency is a product design improvement resulting from (a) marketing research, (b) applied research, (c) pure research, (d) advertising research. .... 3. _____

4. Research in fiber optics conducted for the purpose of increasing the amount of voice and data communications that can move on the same transmission line is an example of (a) pure research, (b) product research, (c) applied research, (d) experimental research. ..... 4. _____

5. Which of the following businesses would be LEAST likely to locate close to the source of raw materials? (a) furniture manufacturer, (b) steel mill, (c) soft drink bottler, (d) all of the businesses listed would need to locate close to sources of raw materials. .... 5. _____

6. The American management expert W. Edwards Deming suggested that the most important goal for businesses is (a) reducing costs, (b) underpricing the competition, (c) effective marketing, (d) quality. .... 6. _____

7. The United States is changing from the world's leading manufacturing economy to the leading (a) marketing economy, (b) agriculture economy, (c) production economy, (d) service economy. .... 7. _____

8. Which of the following is an example of a service business? (a) an equipment rental business, (b) an insurance agency, (c) a home cleaning business, (d) all are examples of service businesses. .... 8. _____

9. A difference between a product and a service is (a) a service is intangible and a product is tangible, (b) a service can be separated from the person supplying it and a product cannot, (c) the quality of a service depends on the manufacturer, (d) a service can be stored or held longer than a product. .... 9. _____

10. Scheduling fewer lifeguards at a swimming pool during a particularly cool summer is an example of (a) matching supply and demand, (b) matching cost and price, (c) overemphasizing personnel decisions, (d) a poor marketing decision. .... 10. _____

Total Score _____

Part C—*Directions:* In the Answers column, write the letter of the word or expression in Column I that most closely matches each statement in Column II.

Column I	Column II	Answers
A. custom manufacturing	1. Short production runs make batches of different products.	_____
B. mass production	2. A large number of products are produced, each of which is identical to the next.	_____
C. continuous processing	3. Raw materials constantly move through equipment that converts them into a more usable form.	_____
D. repetitive production	4. A product is designed and built to meet the specific needs of a purchaser.	_____
E. intermittent processing	5. Modules are assembled in the same way over and over to produce the finished product.	_____

Total Score _____

Name _____

Directions: Study each controversial issue carefully. Follow the advice of your teacher before listing in the columns provided reasons why people might answer Yes or No. Your teacher may want you to work with a class-mate, talk with others in your community to gather information, or use the library or Internet to gather facts.

19-1. If a company's research discovers a way to build a safer product but the change makes the product much more expensive and difficult to use, should the company produce and market the safer product?

Reasons for "Yes"	Reasons for "No"

19-2. If the United States continues to change from a manufacturing economy to a service economy, will wages and the standard of living for most citizens decline?

Reasons for "Yes"	Reasons for "No"

PROBLEMS

19-A. One consumer products firm spent $2,300,000 on research in a recent year. Those dollars were divided among several types of research as follows:

Consumer research	25%
Pure research	40%
Applied research	35%

1. If the company's research budget was 6 percent of the total sales for the year, what was the amount of the company's sales? $ _____

2. Calculate the amount spent on each type of research.

   a. Consumer research $ _____

   b. Pure research $ _____

   c. Applied research $ _____

3. In the space below, construct a bar graph that shows the percentage of the total research budget spent on each type of research.

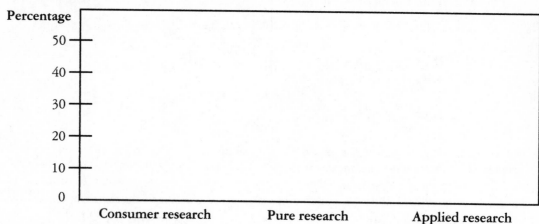

19-B. Jackson and Smith, Inc., is considering building a new factory. It has limited the choice of location to three states. One of the factors the company is considering is the taxes and fees it will have to pay in each state. It has collected the following information:

Tax or Fee	State #1	State #2	State #3
Corporate income tax	3%	6%	10%
Property tax	$35/1,000	$30/1,000	$25/1,000
Annual corporation fee	$1,000	$0	$250
Annual license fees	$100	$1,000	$3,000

If the company plans to build a $6,000,000 plant and estimates a net income the first year of $360,000, compute the total cost of taxes and fees for the first year in each state.

	State #1	State #2	State #3
Corporate income tax	$	$	$
Property tax	$	$	$
Annual corporation fee	$	$	$
Annual license fees	$	$	$
Total	$	$	$

19-C. The Raydon Company is planning an important change in one of its products. Management has identified the following steps that need to be completed and the estimated time it will take to complete each step:

1. Review of old product by consumer panel   14 days
2. Product design   70 days
3. Product development   40 days
4. Developing manufacturing facilities   60 days
5. Test marketing   90 days
6. Production and distribution   30 days

The Raydon Company is beginning the process on March 14. Assume that each step must be completed before the next step is started. Identify the date each step (1–6) will be completed and (7) the earliest date customers will be able to buy the new product.

Step	Date
1.	_____
2.	_____
3.	_____
4.	_____
5.	_____
6.	_____
7.	_____

19-D. You and your friend are planning to start a service business. The business will provide pet and plant care for people while they are on vacation. For each of the following characteristics of service businesses, a customer need is identified. In the column on the right, describe one thing your business will do to ensure that it will be able to meet that specific customer need.

Characteristic	Specific Customer Need	What will your business do to meet that customer need?
1. Form	Some people have exotic plants requiring special care.	
2. Availability	People want to be certain that you will deliver the promised services, so they don't have to worry while on vacation.	
3. Quality	Pet owners want their pets to receive attention and to follow their accustomed schedule.	
4. Timing	Some pet owners need to find a place to leave their pets for an afternoon or evening on very short notice.	

19-E. An automobile manufacturer asked a marketing research firm to survey prospective new car buyers. One of the questions asked the respondents to identify the factor that was most important to them when purchasing a new car. The responses are summarized in the following table:

Factor	Number of Responses	Percent of Total
Price	210	_____ %
Styling	480	_____ %
Brand name	365	_____ %
Reputation of dealer	240	_____ %
Special accessories	245	_____ %
Fuel economy	400	_____ %
Other	60	_____ %
Total respondents	_____	

1. Complete the table by calculating the total number of people responding to the survey and the percentage of respondents who selected each of the factors as most important.
2. After reviewing the results, make two specific, written recommendations to the automobile manufacturer to help in the design of cars for the types of people surveyed.

Recommendation #1:

_____

_____

_____

_____

Recommendation #2:

_____

_____

_____

_____

19-F. Often, to enhance a service business, a company will offer products associated with the service. For each of the service businesses listed below, think of at least one product offered by the business. Write the product on the space provided.

Service Business	Product Offered
1. Dog groomer	_____
2. Hair salon	_____
3. Carpet cleaners	_____
4. Internet service provider	_____
5. Dentist	_____

Conversely, businesses that sell products often offer services to complement their products. Think of at least five products that include a free service. Write your answers on the spaces provided.

Product	Service Provided
1. _____	_____
2. _____	_____
3. _____	_____
4. _____	_____
5. _____	_____

SMALL GROUP ACTIVITIES

Group Activity 1

With instructions from your teacher, divide into groups of four or five students. In your group, read the following scenario and answer the questions.

Companies regularly work to identify new products that they can introduce to consumers. Those products can result from pure or applied research, from the study of consumer needs, and from the recommendations of customers or company employees. Many new product ideas are developed creatively when businesspeople think about problems and needs.

For each of the categories listed below, identify an existing product that appears to have been developed to fit that category. List that product or its description in the second column. Then in the third column, try to develop a new product idea that fits the criteria.

Criteria	Current Product	New Product Idea
1. Making a household task easier	_____	_____
2. A new recreational activity	_____	_____
3. A new use for an old product	_____	_____
4. A product related to a holiday or a special event	_____	_____
5. A product that uses new technology	_____	_____
6. A product that makes it easier to use another product	_____	_____
7. A product designed to reduce the chance of accident or injury	_____	_____

Group Activity 2

With instructions from your teacher, divide into groups so that the number of students per group is equal to the number of groups formed. You are preparing to conduct a customer panel on some aspect of your high school experience. Your teacher will give each group a topic. Spend about 10–15 minutes brainstorming questions to ask about your topic. When your teacher signals time, your group will disburse into new groups made up of one member from each original group. Each person will take turns acting as panel leader and asking the questions for his or her assigned topic to the rest of the group acting as the panel. After everyone has had an opportunity to survey a panel on their topic, the original groups will reconvene and compile, analyze, and summarize results to share with the rest of the class.

<table>
<tr><td rowspan="3">Chapter 20

Nature
and Scope
of Marketing</td><td rowspan="3">Name _____

Date _____</td><td colspan="5" align="center">Scoring Record</td></tr>
<tr><td></td><td>Part A</td><td>Part B</td><td>Part C</td><td>Total</td></tr>
<tr><td>Perfect score</td><td>20</td><td>10</td><td>5</td><td>35</td></tr>
<tr><td></td><td></td><td>My score</td><td></td><td></td><td></td><td></td></tr>
</table>

Study Guide

Part A—*Directions:* Indicate your answer to each of the following questions by writing either yes or no in the Answers column.

Answers

1. Do people make decisions in their daily lives that influence supply and demand? .... 1. _____
2. Do marketing activities help to match production and consumption in our private enterprise economy? .... 2. _____
3. Is marketing defined as the transporting of products from producers to consumers? .... 3. _____
4. Are retailers and wholesalers involved in marketing? .... 4. _____
5. Are jobs that involve customer service and credit services types of marketing jobs? .... 5. _____
6. Does approximately half of every dollar consumers spend go to pay the cost of marketing activities? .... 6. _____
7. Do firms that are production oriented pay most attention to decisions about what and how to produce? .... 7. _____
8. Do firms that are customer oriented emphasize widespread distribution and promotion in order to sell the products produced? .... 8. _____
9. Should a company that has adopted the marketing concept have a marketing manager as a part of top management? .... 9. _____
10. Does selecting a market involve determining whom to serve and where to serve? .... 10. _____
11. Is a good target market made up of people with very diverse needs and wants? .... 11. _____
12. Do marketers group customers by characteristics such as age, gender, family status, education, income, and occupation? .... 12. _____
13. Is the marketing mix a blend of all decisions related to the four elements of marketing? 13. _____
14. Do companies that market the same product usually use the same marketing mix? .... 14. _____
15. Is a product most profitable during the introductory stage of the product life cycle? .... 15. _____
16. Can some companies move a product out of the decline stage of the product life cycle by finding new uses for the product? .... 16. _____
17. Can the same product be both an industrial good and a consumer good? .... 17. _____
18. Do consumers believe that most brands of shopping goods are quite similar? .... 18. _____
19. Are unsought goods products that consumers do not shop for because they feel no strong need for them? .... 19. _____
20. Do many of the complaints consumers have about businesses today involve marketing activities? .... 20. _____

Total Score _____

Part B—*Directions:* For each of the following statements, select the word, or group of words, that best completes the statement. In the Answers column, write the letter corresponding to the answer selected.

1. The goal of effective marketing is to (a) create and maintain satisfying exchange relationships, (b) successfully sell the products produced, (c) find the right price to make a profit, (d) distribute products as efficiently as possible. .... 1. _____

2. What percentage of all people employed in the United States work in a marketing job or a marketing business? (a) less than 10 percent, (b) well over 33 percent, (c) about 50 percent, (d) nearly 90 percent. .... 2. _____

3. Which of the major marketing activities is involved in holding goods until they are needed by consumers? (a) buying, (b) transporting, (c) storing, (d) grading and valuing. 3. _____

4. An attractive market is one that has (a) few existing competitors, (b) a large number of customers with a need for the product, (c) customers with sufficient money to spend on such a product, (d) all of these. .... 4. _____

5. Companies that direct their activities at satisfying the needs of consumers are (a) customer oriented, (b) sales oriented, (c) production oriented, (d) competition oriented. .... 5. _____

6. Groups of customers with similar needs are known as (a) final consumers, (b) industrial consumers, (c) marketing mixes, (d) target markets. .... 6. _____

7. If you bought a computer, which of the following items that came with your computer could be considered part of the product? (a) the hard drive, (b) the software installed on it, (c) the technical support provided by the company, (d) all of these are part of the product. 7. _____

8. Which of the following is NOT an element of the marketing mix? (a) people, (b) product, (c) place, (d) price. .... 8. _____

9. The product life cycle stage in which sales are highest is (a) introduction, (b) growth, (c) maturity, (d) decline. .... 9. _____

10. Whether a product is an industrial good or a consumer good is based on (a) who uses the product, (b) what kind of company makes the product, (c) the type of marketing activities used, (d) the price of the product. .... 10. _____

Total Score _____

Part C—*Directions:* In the Answers column, write the letter of the word or expression in Column I that most closely matches each statement in Column II.

Column I	Column II	Answers
A. convenience goods	1. Products used by another business.	_____
B. industrial goods	2. Products among which consumers see important differences in terms of prices and features of different brands.	_____
C. shopping goods	3. Products that many consumers do not feel a strong need for, such as life insurance, encyclopedias, and funeral services.	
D. specialty goods		_____
E. unsought goods	4. Inexpensive items that consumers purchase regularly.	_____
	5. Particular products that consumers insist on having and are willing to search for.	_____
	Total Score	_____

Name _____

Directions: Study each controversial issue carefully. Follow the advice of your teacher before listing in the columns provided reasons why people might answer Yes or No. Your teacher may want you to work with a classmate, talk with others in your community to gather information, or use the library or Internet to gather facts.

20-1. Does marketing cause people to purchase products and services they really don't want or need?

Reasons for "Yes"	Reasons for "No"

20-2. Are most businesses today customer oriented?

Reasons for "Yes"	Reasons for "No"

PROBLEMS

20-A. Marketing-oriented firms attempt to identify target markets before they sell their products. For most products, there will be several groups of potential customers. Each group will have different needs and will want a different marketing mix.

For each of the products listed below, describe two unique target markets for the product. Then describe the marketing mix that would be needed to satisfy each of the target markets.

Product	Description of Target Market	Description of Marketing Mix
Automobile	#1	
	#2	
Motel	#1	
	#2	

20-B. Marketing managers make decisions about each of the elements of the marketing mix—product, price, promotion, and place. For each of the marketing decisions listed below, decide which element is most related to the decision. Place a check mark in the appropriate column to indicate your answer.

Marketing Decision	Product	Price	Promotion	Place
1. A new package will be used for the product.	___	___	___	___
2. We will sell two albums for $12.	___	___	___	___
3. A display of the new shoes will be built inside the store entrance.	___	___	___	___
4. A discount of 2 percent will be given if payment is received within 30 days.	___	___	___	___
5. We will begin advertising our product on television.	___	___	___	___
6. A wholesaler will sell the product to retailers.	___	___	___	___
7. If the goods are sent by air, they will get to the store sooner.	___	___	___	___
8. We must improve the quality to satisfy the customer.	___	___	___	___
9. We will open a store in the new shopping center.	___	___	___	___
10. We will provide more training for our salespeople.	___	___	___	___

20-C. Some goods are marketed directly from the producer to the consumer. Ask your relatives and neighbors what purchases they have recently made directly from the producer. Report in the following space those items purchased and place a check mark in the appropriate column to indicate the method used.

Item Purchased	By Mail or Internet	By Going to the Producer	By Having the Producer or a Salesperson Come to the Consumer
1. _____	___	___	___
2. _____	___	___	___
3. _____	___	___	___
4. _____	___	___	___
5. _____	___	___	___
6. _____	___	___	___

20-D. In a survey of 400 business executives, the respondents identified the marketing activities that were performed in their businesses. The activities and the number of executives who said the activity was performed in their businesses are:

Marketing Activity	Number of Businesses in Which It Is Performed
Buying	341
Selling	386
Transporting	236
Storing	337
Financing	222
Researching	163
Risk taking	332
Grading and valuing	342

1. List the marketing activities in rank order according to the number of firms that perform each activity:

a. _____   e. _____

b. _____   f. _____

c. _____   g. _____

d. _____   h. _____

2. How many additional firms are involved in storing activities than are involved in financing activities? _____

3. What percentage of total firms are involved in risk-taking activities? _____

4. What percentage of the firms conduct research as a part of their marketing efforts? _____

5. Why do you believe that the highest-rated marketing activity is selling, while research is the lowest-rated activity? _____

_____

_____

20-E. For each of the following descriptions of competition, identify whether the product is in the introduction, growth, maturity, or decline stage of the product life cycle.

Description	Life-Cycle Stage
1. Several brands of a product are available, and new brands are being introduced. Profits are excellent for the brands already on the market.	_____
2. A company is attempting to improve its product. It is losing sales because a new, much-improved product has been introduced by a competitor. Sales are not very good, and many competitors are losing money.	_____
3. Many customers have purchased the product and find it to be quite satisfying. Because of a very profitable market in the past, many businesses have brands that are competing for a share of the market. The companies spend a great deal of money on promotion, but customers are not very loyal to one brand.	_____
4. Some customers are excited about a new product that they believe offers real advantages compared to other products they have been buying. However, only one brand is currently available, and it is very high priced—so most customers continue to buy the products they are used to. If the company cannot find new customers quickly, it will be unable to make a profit.	_____
5. Sales are the highest they have ever been in the market, but companies are having a difficult time making a profit. Costs are increasing as companies try hard to convince customers that their brand is best. It seems that while businesses work hard to attract customers, the customers really don't seem to recognize important differences among the many brands.	_____

20-F. Products can be classified as either industrial or consumer goods, depending on who buys the product and how they will use it. It is also possible for the same product to fit within any of the four consumer goods classifications, depending on how important the product is to the consumers and whether they are willing to shop and compare products and brands. In the Answers column, write the letter of the goods classification in Column I that most closely matches each product use description in Column II.

I. Goods Classification	II. Description of Product Use	Answers
A. industrial good B. convenience good C. shopping good D. specialty good E. unsought good	1. A recent college graduate has saved enough money to make a down payment on a new car. She will be able to afford a car of no more than $11,000. In order to make the best decision, she reads a popular consumer magazine that rates the major brands. She asks several coworkers about their experiences with three brands she is considering. When she has decided on a model, she visits two dealers to compare prices.	_____
	2. An insurance company is replacing ten cars in its fleet. The purchasing agent contacts three manufacturers and provides specifications for the ten cars. When bids are received, the company selects the lowest bid and makes the purchase.	_____
	3. A 50-year-old man has purchased a new car every four years for the past twenty years. He used to spend a great deal of time shopping and comparing and was not brand loyal. However, he has been quite satisfied with his last two cars, which were both the same brand. So this year he has decided to go to his local dealer and buy the latest model of that brand.	_____
	4. A mother is filling her shopping cart at the grocery store. She needs to buy diapers and wipes for her baby. She has been satisfied with the brand she normally buys, and she can't see any particular difference between her brand and others, so she just grabs her usual brand and heads for the checkout line.	_____
	5. A college student has just moved to a new apartment that is five miles from campus. To get to campus for classes, most students choose to ride a bicycle, take the bus, or drive an automobile. Because the student does not have a garage or parking space, she decides it will be most convenient to ride the bus each day.	_____

SMALL GROUP ACTIVITIES

Group Activity 1

With instructions from your teacher, divide into groups of four or five students. Your group is assigned the job of coming up with an idea for a fund-raising activity for your school. After you have decided on the activity, your task is to plan how you will market the fund-raising activity, using all four elements of the marketing mix. Be prepared to present your ideas to the class.

Group Activity 2

With instructions from your teacher, divide into groups of four or five students. Complete the following chart, describing the marketing activities that must completed for each product or service listed and, if possible, who is responsible for completing each activity. Be prepared to present your list to the class.

Marketing Activity	Crest® Toothpaste	Alpo® Dog Food	Gold's Gym®	American Airlines®
Buying				
Selling				
Transporting				
Storing				
Financing				
Researching				
Risk taking				
Grading and valuing				

Chapter 21		Scoring Record				
Product Development and Distribution	Name _____ Date _____		**Part A**	**Part B**	**Part C**	**Total**
		Perfect score	20	10	10	40
		My score				

Study Guide

Part A—*Directions:* Indicate your answer to each of the following questions by writing either yes or no in the Answers column.

		Answers
1.	Do businesspeople and consumers have the same perceptions of a product?	1. _____
2.	Do businesses study their target markets to decide what basic, enhanced, and extended products to produce?	2. _____
3.	If a business decides to offer its product in a variety of sizes, would it be expanding its product line?	3. _____
4.	If consumers are satisfied with one product from a company, are they likely to have confidence in a different product sold under the same brand?	4. _____
5.	Does our economic system rely on the successful exchange of products and services between businesses and consumers?	5. _____
6.	Do differences between the offerings of businesses and the requirements of consumers create an economic discrepancy?	6. _____
7.	Are businesses that participate in activities that transfer goods and services from the producer to the user called marketing channels?	7. _____
8.	Are producers and consumers the most common types of channel members?	8. _____
9.	Does the shortest distribution channel include a retailer?	9. _____
10.	Will a manufacturer need fewer salespeople if a channel of distribution includes retailers rather than going directly to consumers?	10. _____
11.	Is it illegal to have more than one wholesaler in a channel of distribution?	11. _____
12.	Does one business own the organizations at other levels of a channel of distribution in an administered channel?	12. _____
13.	Is it possible for the same product to be sold through several different channels of distribution at the same time?	13. _____
14.	Will the channel of distribution usually be short for a product that requires special handling?	14. _____
15.	Are railroads responsible for handling over half of the volume of products shipped in the United States?	15. _____
16.	Are trucks frequently used for short-distance shipping?	16. _____
17.	Is air shipping used primarily for small, high value, or perishable items?	17. _____
18.	Though air transport is one of the most expensive means of transporting goods, are more products continually being shipped by air?	18. _____
19.	Can the bar codes on products and packages be used to track the products during shipment?	19. _____
20.	Is a distribution center a building used to store large quantities of products until they can be sold?	20. _____

Total Score _____

Part B—*Directions:* For each of the following statements, select the word, or group of words, that best completes the statement. In the Answers column, write the letter corresponding to the answer selected.

1. Which of the following is NOT one of the levels of product design? (a) extended product, (b) basic product, (c) expanded product, (d) enhanced product. .... 1. _____

2. An extended product is (a) the physical product in its simplest form, (b) a product that offers different features and options for the consumer, (c) a product that includes additional features that are not part of the physical product, (d) both a and b. .... 2. _____

3. A group of similar products with obvious variations in the design and quality is a (a) basic product, (b) product line, (c) enhanced product, (d) tangible product. .... 3. _____

4. Two important product mix decisions are (a) packaging and branding, (b) pricing and advertising, (c) size and location, (d) transportation and storage. .... 4. _____

5. A brand (a) always indicates quality, (b) often plays a major role in buying decisions, (c) helps protect a product from breakage, (d) makes a product easier to use. .... 5. _____

6. An example of an economic discrepancy is (a) a farmer harvests tomatoes and sells them immediately to customers at a roadside stand, (b) a small furniture manufacturer produces only the products that customers order, (c) a bank is open from 9 a.m. to 5 p.m. but many customers do not get off work until 5:30 p.m., (d) all of these are economic discrepancies. 6. _____

7. Which type of channel member primarily works with other channel members rather than with the final consumer? (a) producer, (b) wholesaler, (c) retailer, (d) end user. .... 7. _____

8. Which of the following is an example of a direct channel of distribution? (a) producer to retailer, (b) retailer to consumer, (c) producer to consumer, (d) wholesaler to retailer. .... 8. _____

9. Combining telephone sales with computer technology is a popular method of direct sales known as (a) telemarketing, (b) computer sales, (c) infomercials, (d) teledistribution. ...... 9. _____

10. A channel of distribution in which one organization takes a leadership position to benefit all channel members is (a) a direct channel, (b) an administered channel, (c) an integrated channel, (d) none of these. .... 10. _____

Total Score _____

Part C—*Directions:* Complete each sentence by filling in the missing word or words.

1. A _____ consists of all attributes, both _____ and _____ that customers receive in exchange for the purchase price.

2. A _____ is the complete set of all products a business offers to a market. It can have _____, _____, or both.

3. When a producer cannot or chooses not to perform all of the marketing activities, the need for an _____ channel of distribution arises.

4. The most commonly used methods of transporting goods are by railroad, _____, and _____.

5. A _____ is a large building designed to accumulate and redistribute products efficiently.

Total Score _____

Directions: Study each controversial issue carefully. Follow the advice of your teacher before listing in the columns provided reasons why people might answer Yes or No. Your teacher may want you to work with a classmate, talk with others in your community to gather information, or use the library or Internet to gather facts.

21-1. Have manufacturers/producers exceeded reasonable limits in offering a wide variety of products and services?

Reasons for "Yes"	Reasons for "No"

21-2. Do wholesalers deserve some type of government protection to keep them from being forced out of channels of distribution by large producers or retailers?

Reasons for "Yes"	Reasons for "No"

PROBLEMS

21-A. For the following products and services, complete the chart below describing the features of the basic product, enhanced product, and extended product. The first row is filled in as an example.

Product	Basic Features	Enhanced Features	Extended Features
Car wash service	Wash and wax	Vacuuming, air freshener	Services in your driveway, detailing
Refrigerator			
Automobile			
Dog grooming service			
Fitness center			
Personal computer			

21-B. A brand is a name, symbol, word, or design that identifies a product, service, or company. Although producers want customers to make pleasant associations with their brands, sometimes brands help customers avoid undesired products and services. Based on your shopping experience, list five brands that you use regularly and five brands that you usually choose not to purchase. List reasons for your answers.

Brands I Purchase   **Reasons**

1. _____   _____

2. _____   _____

3. _____   _____

4. _____   _____

5. _____   _____

Brands I Avoid   **Reasons**

1. _____   _____

2. _____   _____

3. _____   _____

4. _____   _____

5. _____   _____

21-C. A channel member is often used to reduce the number of transactions that must occur in a channel of distribution. The charts below show how including a retailer reduces the number of transactions needed to move products between producers and consumers.

1. Draw lines between the producers and consumers in the following chart to show the transactions that must occur if each consumer buys each producer's product. Two transactions are shown as examples.

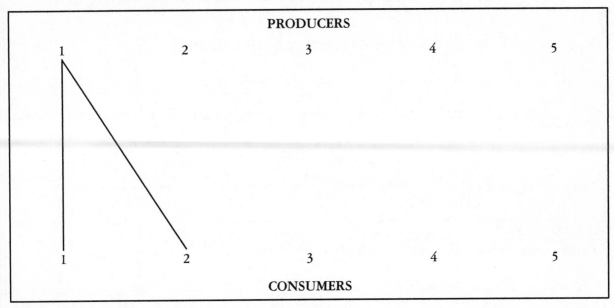

2. Draw lines indicating the transactions that need to be made if a retailer is used. Each consumer again buys every product, and all products are sold by the retailer. An example is shown for two transactions.

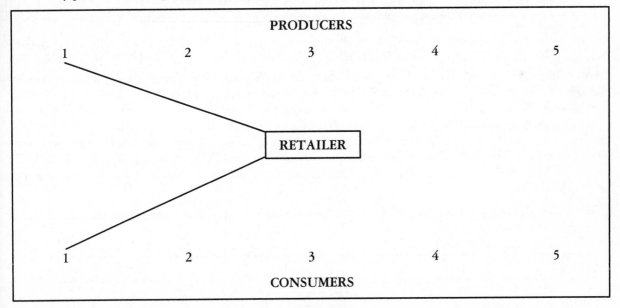

3. How many transactions were needed when no retailer was present? _____

4. How many transactions were needed when the retailer was used? _____

5. In addition to reducing the number of buying and selling transactions, what benefits result from the retailer entering the marketing channel? _____

_____

_____

_____

21-D. A manufacturer regularly makes shipments to a retailer located 800 miles away. The shipment weighs 50 pounds. The following chart shows the cost of shipment using several methods.

Carrier	Cost
Bus	$18.75
Parcel service	9.50
Air freight	42.00
Truck	28.50

1. Why are there such differences in the cost of shipping the same package?

_____

_____

_____

_____

_____

2. Describe a situation in which a manufacturer may choose to use air freight to ship a package.

_____

_____

3. Assume the manufacturer ships one package each week. In a one-year period, what is the difference in the shipping costs between the highest and lowest cost method?

_____

21-E. A small business will soon open to produce high-quality leather wallets, purses, and related accessories. For at least the first three years of the business, the owners plan to sell the products only within a 50-mile radius of the business's location. The owners are trying to decide on the most appropriate distribution channel and are evaluating three choices: (1) They would open one retail outlet in a large shopping center located ten miles from the business and sell directly to customers through that store. (2) They would hire a manufacturer's agent, who would contact retailers in the area and try to get the retail stores to add the company's products to their inventories. (3) They would hire several people to call area retailers using telemarketing to encourage the retailers to order the products.

1. In the space below, draw a diagram of each of the three trade channels described above, using Figure 21-3 in your textbook as an example.

Trade Channel #1

Trade Channel #2

Trade Channel #3

2. Write a brief statement describing each channel.

Trade Channel #1:

_____

_____

_____

_____

Trade Channel #2:

_____

_____

_____

Trade Channel #3:

_____

_____

_____

_____

SMALL GROUP ACTIVITIES

Group Activity 1

With instructions from your teacher, divide into small groups and answer the following questions.

A company that operates a distribution center is considering the purchase of an automated product-storage system. The system moves packages on metal tracks to storage bins through the use of robots that load and unload the packages from the bins. The system will cost $380,000 and will require two people to operate it. It is expected that the salary of each of the two people will average $25,000 a year.

Currently, packages in the distribution system are handled by 15 employees using handcarts. Each employee has a handcart, which costs $100 each and must be replaced every three years. The average employee salary is $15,000 a year.

1. Using only equipment and employee costs, compare the company's costs of the automated system and the current system for the next four years. Assume that the company will buy each employee a new handcart in Year 1.

Year	Automated System	Current System
1	$ _____	$ _____
2	$ _____	$ _____
3	$ _____	$ _____
4	$ _____	$ _____
Total cost	$ _____	$ _____

2. In addition to the equipment and employee costs, list four other factors the company should consider in deciding whether to purchase the automated system.

1. _____

2. _____

3. _____

4. _____

Group Activity 2

With directions from your teacher, divide into groups and answer the following questions.

Identify three retail stores in your community that fit into each of the categories listed below. Then describe the differences you found among the categories of retail stores. Be prepared to share your choices with the class.

A store that offers a broad variety of many products:

_____   _____   _____

A store that offers a large variety of a few products:

_____   _____   _____

A store that offers many products with limited variety:

_____   _____   _____

A store that offers limited products and variety:

_____   _____   _____

Study Guide

Part A—*Directions:* Indicate your answer to each of the following questions by writing either yes or no in the Answers column.

Answers

1. Should products be priced so that buyers consider them a good value for the money? ...... 1. _____

2. Are these the four decisions businesses must make when planning a purchase: what to purchase, when to purchase, how much to purchase, and what to do with the goods after the purchase? .... 2. _____

3. Are customers' needs the most important consideration for businesses when they make purchases? .... 3. _____

4. Do companies that sell to other businesses often extend credit to their customers? .... 4. _____

5. Are discounts offered by suppliers to their business customers subtracted from the selling price? .... 5. _____

6. For a product, is the price charged to the final consumer the cost of goods sold? .... 6. _____

7. Is markup the same as profit? .... 7. _____

8. Does setting an extremely high price for a product ensure a profit for the business? .... 8. _____

9. When stated in dollars and cents, are markup and margin identical? .... 9. _____

10. Does a business determine the price that will earn a specific profit by adding the costs of producing the product to the target profit? .... 10. _____

11. Is promotion the primary marketing activity used to communicate with prospective customers? .... 11. _____

12. Does advertising include both paid and nonpaid promotion? .... 12. _____

13. Is more money spent on advertising in the United States each year than is spent on any other type of promotion? .... 13. _____

14. Are billboards a type of mass-media advertising? .... 14. _____

15. Would a business with a loyal group of customers and a product that has been on the market a long time likely have to spend more money on advertising than a new business with a very complex product? .... 15. _____

16. Should salespeople deal with all customers in the same way when selling the company's products and services? .... 16. _____

17. Are amusement, friendship, and fear all examples of buying motives? .... 17. _____

18. Should salespeople discourage customers from handling or using the product to avoid damage or injury? .... 18. _____

19. Should a salesperson encourage a customer to ask questions and identify any objections during the sales presentation? .... 19. _____

20. Are coupons an effective method of increasing a product's sales for a short period of time? 20. _____

Total Score _____

Part B—*Directions:* For each of the following statements, select the word, or group of words, that best completes the statement. In the Answers column, write the letter corresponding to the answer selected.

1. The business buying decision includes (a) what and when to purchase, (b) from whom to purchase, (c) how much to purchase, (d) all of these. ....

   1. _____

2. A discount given to the buyer for ordering or taking delivery of goods in advance of the normal buying period is a (a) quantity discount, (b) cash discount, (c) seasonal discount, (d) trade discount. ....

   2. _____

3. If a product sells for $40, the operating expenses are $23, and the cost of goods sold is $24, what is the net profit or loss? (a) a loss of $7, (b) a profit of $87, (c) a profit of $1, (d) a profit of $17. ....

   3. _____

4. If customers carefully compare prices among several businesses, a business should probably use which method of pricing? (a) pricing to meet competition, (b) pricing to earn a specific profit, (c) pricing based on consumer demand, (d) pricing to sell more merchandise. ....

   4. _____

5. The primary difference between advertising and selling is that advertising is (a) expensive, (b) impersonal, (c) able to reach fewer people at one time, (d) all of these are differences between advertising and selling. ....

   5. _____

6. Which of the following is NOT a form of advertising media? (a) publications, (b) mass media, (c) salespeople, (d) displays. ....

   6. _____

7. A large one-time expenditure for advertising should be used when the business (a) has very little money, (b) is promoting a successful product, (c) has a great deal of competition, (d) is introducing a new product. ....

   7. _____

8. For many salespeople, the most difficult part of the selling process is (a) presenting and demonstrating the product, (b) answering customer questions, (c) closing the sale, (d) suggestion selling. ....

   8. _____

9. Window displays, layouts for newspaper advertisements, and sales presentation materials provided by manufacturers to retailers are all examples of (a) publicity, (b) dealer aids, (c) advertising support, (d) promotional materials. ....

   9. _____

10. The legal requirement that advertisers be able to prove their claims about their products is called (a) corrective advertising, (b) cease and desist order, (c) substantiation, (d) full disclosure. ....

    10. _____

Total Score _____

Part C—*Directions:* In the Answers column, write the letter of the word or expression in Column I that most closely matches each statement in Column II.

Column I	Column II	Answers
A. cash discount	1. The actual price customers pay for the product or service	_____
B. cost of goods sold	2. The difference between the selling price and all costs and expenses of the business	_____
C. net profit		
D. selling price	3. A price reduction that manufacturers give to their channel partners in exchange for additional services	_____
E. trade discount	4. The cost to produce the product or buy it for resale	_____
	5. A price reduction given for paying by a certain date	_____
	Total Score	_____

Directions: Study each controversial issue carefully. Follow the advice of your teacher before listing in the columns provided reasons why people might answer Yes or No. Your teacher may want you to work with a classmate, talk with others in your community to gather information, or use the library or Internet to gather facts.

22-1. If a business is facing increasing prices and inflation, should it cut the quality of the products and services sold in order to prevent major increases in the prices it charges to customers?

Reasons for "Yes"	Reasons for "No"

22-2. Returned merchandise represents a major cost for businesses, which they often pass on to consumers in the form of higher prices. Should businesses tighten up their rules for returning merchandise to help control costs?

Reasons for "Yes"	Reasons for "No"

PROBLEMS

22-A. One of the problems of operating a retail business is deciding how many brands of an item should be stocked. Before making a decision, managers like to know how many different brands and sizes are stocked by competing business firms. Visit a supermarket and a small convenience store and count the number of brands and different package sizes stocked for each item listed below. Record your answers in the appropriate spaces on the form.

Item	Supermarket		Convenience Store	
	Number of Brands	Number of Package Sizes	Number of Brands	Number of Package Sizes
Sugar				
Canned peaches				
Frozen pizza				
Gelatin dessert				
Milk				

1. Why do you believe there are differences in the number of brands and package sizes carried by the supermarket and the convenience store? _____

_____

_____

_____

2. Why do you believe that more brands and package sizes are available for some products than for others?

_____

_____

_____

_____

22-B. A store that sells children's clothing had 120 items returned during one season.

Number of Items Returned	Reasons	Percent of Total
40	Wrong size	_____
10	Child did not like it	_____
3	Defective merchandise	_____
45	Shrunk when washed	_____
20	Changed mind	_____
2	Salesperson gave incorrect information	_____
Total 120		100%

1. Complete the chart by determining the percentage of total returned items represented by each of the reasons.

2. If you were the owner of this store, what might you do to reduce the number of returns?

_____

_____

22-C. Calculate the missing amounts in the chart:

Cost of Merchandise	Operating Expenses	Markup	Net Profit	% Markup on Cost	Selling Price
$ 34.00	$12.00	$_____	$ 2.00	_____	$_____
1.20	_____	1.20	0.07	_____	_____
_____	7.50	_____	2.50	_____	13.50
_____	62.75	85.55	_____	_____	327.95
0.60	0.25	0.30	_____	_____	_____
6.00	2.50	_____	_____	66.66%	_____

22-D. Most businesses provide accurate and honest information to prospective customers when advertising and selling products. Businesspeople know that if customers discover that purchases were made as a result of incorrect or inaccurate information, those customers will be dissatisfied and probably will not buy from the business again. However, a few businesses continue to use unethical practices in advertising and selling. Five advertisements used by unethical businesses are summarized below. For each advertisement, explain why it is unfair and misleading to consumers.

1. An advertisement of a year-end sale says, "Everything in the store reduced." However, many of the most popular items are not put on sale. _____

   _____

   _____

2. An advertisement for toothpaste tells prospective buyers that another company's toothpaste is inferior to the advertiser's product. However, there is no proof of the advertised claims. _____

   _____

   _____

3. A baseball player is used in a testimonial for a brand of auto tires. The player had never used the tires before the advertisement was made. _____

   _____

   _____

4. An advertisement for furniture says, "Three rooms of furniture for $200." The furniture is of poor construction and is mismatched or out of date. The ad gives no information on quality or style. _____

   _____

   _____

5. A stereo company sends an announcement to people telling them they have won a free stereo. When the winners come into the store to claim their prize, they are not allowed to take it unless they sign a contract to buy 200 compact discs at very high prices. _____

   _____

   _____

22-E. Do you have the characteristics necessary to be a good salesperson? While it is difficult to identify what makes a good salesperson, some personal characteristics are very important. Rate yourself on the following checklist to see how many of the characteristics you already have. Be honest with yourself. Place a check mark in the column that best describes you.

Personal Characteristics	Usually	Sometimes	Seldom
1. I am concerned about the feelings of others.	____	____	____
2. I take time to help others when they have problems.	____	____	____
3. I listen to other people without interrupting.	____	____	____
4. I believe other people's opinions are as important as mine.	____	____	____
5. I am a happy person.	____	____	____
6. I enjoy the things I do.	____	____	____
7. I think most of my problems can be solved.	____	____	____
8. I like to learn about things—how they are made and how they work.	____	____	____
9. When I meet people, I try to learn their names and something about them.	____	____	____
10. I like to talk to people about themselves, not about me.	____	____	____
11. I don't like to hurt other people's feelings.	____	____	____
12. I can say the right thing at the right time.	____	____	____
13. I work at a task I enjoy until it is completed.	____	____	____
14. I like to plan my day before I begin it.	____	____	____
15. I am good at solving problems when they occur.	____	____	____
16. I am concerned about the way other people think I look.	____	____	____
17. When I talk with people, they understand what I say.	____	____	____
18. When I tell people something, they can believe me.	____	____	____
19. If I promise to do something, I follow through.	____	____	____
20. Friendship and trust are important to me.	____	____	____

If most of your check marks are in the Usually column, you already have many of the personal characteristics needed by salespeople. If you checked Sometimes or Seldom on some items, you may consider ways to improve in those areas and create plans for self-improvement.

22-F. Some companies plan the amount they will spend on advertising by developing an estimate of the sales for the year and then setting the advertising budget as a percentage of the estimated sales. In the following table, Column 1 lists the planned sales for the year, and Column 2 provides the percentage of sales the company plans to spend on advertising. Calculate each company's advertising budget by completing Column 3.

Column 4 lists the actual sales achieved by each company during the year, and Column 5 shows the actual amount spent on advertising for the year. Calculate the percentage of sales actually spent on advertising by each firm by completing Column 6.

Firm	Column 1 Budgeted Sales	Column 2 Advertising Percent	Column 3 Budgeted Advertising	Column 4 Actual Sales	Column 5 Actual Advertising	Column 6 Advertising Percent
A	$ 950,000	3.0%	$ _____	$1,100,000	$ 32,000	_____
B	230,000	11.0%	_____	210,000	25,500	_____
C	6,600,000	1.5%	_____	6,950,000	105,500	_____
D	155,250	10.0%	_____	158,000	15,800	_____
E	2,850,500	5.5%	_____	2,860,000	171,600	_____

SMALL GROUP ACTIVITIES

Group Activity 1

With the help of your teacher, divide into groups of three to five students to work on the following problem.

1. Some types of products are most effectively sold through full-service stores where customers can receive help from knowledgeable salespeople. Others can be sold easily through self-service merchandising. In your groups, review the following list of products. For those that typically would require full-service selling, place an F in the blank space after the item. For those that could be effectively sold through self-service merchandising, place an S in the blank space.

Product	Full or Self-Service	Store
Automobiles	F	CarMax
Diamond rings		
Magazines		
Camera lenses		
Fresh fruits and vegetables		
Children's games		
Television sets		
School supplies		

2. Together, write a brief explanation for why your group feels it is possible to sell the items you marked with an S with self-service merchandising, while the other items will require full-service selling.

3. Retail stores are constantly changing. Relying on the personal experience and knowledge of all group members, think of either a full-service store that would sell the product you indicated as self-service or a self-service store that would sell the product you indicated was full-service. Place your answers in the third column of the table. An example is provided to help you get started.

Group Activity 2

In groups of three to five students, consider the following problem.

Individuals are motivated to buy for different reasons. Some common buying motives are listed on the next page. For each buying motive in the column on the left, your group should think of one product and one service that someone would buy as a result of that motive. An example is provided for you.

Be prepared to share your answers with the class.

Name _____

Buying Motive	Product	Service
Status	Mercedes Benz automobile	House cleaning service
Appetite	_____	_____
Comfort	_____	_____
Desire for bargains	_____	_____
Recognition	_____	_____
Ease of use	_____	_____
Love of beauty	_____	_____
Amusement	_____	_____
Desire for good health	_____	_____
Friendship	_____	_____
Affection	_____	_____
Wealth	_____	_____
Enjoyment	_____	_____
Pride of ownership	_____	_____
Fear	_____	_____

Chapter 23		Scoring Record				
Managing Human Resources	Name _____		Part A	Part B	Part C	Total
		Perfect score	20	10	5	35
	Date _____	My score				

Study Guide

Part A—*Directions:* Indicate your answer to each of the following questions by writing either yes or no in the Answers column.

1. Of all the resources used by a business, are people the most important to the success of the business? .... 1. _____

2. Are human resources managers the only managers who work with people? .... 2. _____

3. Are recruiting, hiring, promoting, and firing employees a part of the employment function of human resources management? .... 3. _____

4. Are employee relations activities more formal in companies that have labor unions? .... 4. _____

5. Are human resources personnel responsible for evaluating the performance of each employee and using the results of the evaluations to improve performance? .... 5. _____

6. Do employee assistance programs often help employees with nonwork-related problems? 6. _____

7. Is the first step in hiring a new employee establishing the need for a new hire? .... 7. _____

8. Should companies normally give current employees the first opportunity to apply for open positions in the company? .... 8. _____

9. Do federal laws prevent job applicants from using the Internet to submit their resumes to prospective employers? .... 9. _____

10. Is it a good practice to allow work teams to interview job applicants who may become a part of the team? .... 10. _____

11. To be legal, must tests administered to job applicants measure only characteristics important for success on the job? .... 11. _____

12. Is transferring an employee to another job generally a form of punishment? .... 12. _____

13. Is employee turnover valuable to a company because it provides the opportunity to hire new employees? .... 13. _____

14. Is the Department of Labor the main federal agency that administers and enforces employment laws and workplace safety? .... 14. _____

15. Must companies covered by the Fair Labor Standards Act pay employees overtime pay of 1½ times their regular wage rate? .... 15. _____

16. Are there provisions under Social Security law that allow people to actually receive benefits before they reach retirement age? .... 16. _____

17. Do self-employed people have the same rate for contributions to Social Security and Medicare as an employee of a company? .... 17. _____

18. Are unemployment insurance programs managed by the federal government? .... 18. _____

19. Are employers legally required to make reasonable accommodations to support the employment of disabled employees? .... 19. _____

20. Have companies that have taken steps to increase diversity and reduce discrimination found that the practices benefit business performance? .... 20. _____

Total Score _____

Part B—*Directions:* For each of the following statements, select the word, or group of words, that best completes the statement. In the Answers column, write the letter corresponding to the answer selected.

1. Human resources activities include (a) employment, (b) wages and benefits, (c) performance improvement, (d) all of these activities. .... 1. _____

2. A list of the basic tasks that make up a job is known as a(n) (a) employment application, (b) job specification, (c) job description, (d) performance evaluation. .... 2. _____

3. The first step in processing applicants for a job is (a) interviewing the applicants, (b) reviewing applications to eliminate unqualified applicants, (c) checking an applicant's references, (d) administering knowledge and skill tests. .... 3. _____

4. The advancement of an employee within a company to a position with more authority and responsibility is (a) employee turnover, (b) an employee transfer, (c) a promotion, (d) a layoff. .... 4. _____

5. The extent to which people enter and leave employment in a business during a year is known as (a) layoffs, (b) the application process, (c) transfers and terminations, (d) employee turnover. .... 5. _____

6. Businesses that actively recruit, evaluate, and help people prepare for and locate jobs are (a) employee assistance companies, (b) training agencies, (c) employment agencies, (d) advertising agencies. .... 6. _____

7. As a final step in the employment process, the human resources department should (a) complete a follow-up to see if the right employee was hired, (b) require a physical and drug test, (c) remove the files of all applicants not hired, (d) revise the job description for the new applicant. .... 7. _____

8. Most managers and other types of salaried employees are exempt from the regulations of (a) Social Security, (b) Medicare, (c) the Americans with Disabilities Act (ADA), (d) the Fair Labor Standards Act (FLSA). .... 8. _____

9. Supplemental health insurance for retirement-age people as well as others with specified disabilities is provided through (a) Social Security, (b) Medicare, (c) unemployment insurance, (d) the Americans with Disabilities Act (ADA). .... 9. _____

10. The Age Discrimination in Employment Act prohibits discrimination in conditions of employment or job opportunities for (a) people over the age of 40, (b) teenagers, (c) legal immigrants to the United States, (d) people with disabilities. .... 10. _____

Total Score _____

Part C—*Directions:* In the Answers column, write the letter of the word or expression in Column I that most closely matches each statement in Column II.

Column I	Column II	Answers
A. discharge	1. A temporary or permanent reduction in the number of employees because of a change in business conditions	_____
B. layoff		
C. promotion	2. The advancement of an employee within a company to a position with more authority and responsibility	_____
D. transfer		
E. turnover	3. The rate at which people enter and leave employment in a business during a year	_____
	4. The release of an employee from the company due to inappropriate work behavior	_____
	5. The assignment of an employee to another job in the company that involves the same types of responsibilities and authority	_____

Total Score _____

Name _____

Directions: Study each controversial issue carefully. Follow the advice of your teacher before listing in the columns provided reasons why people might answer Yes or No. Your teacher may want you to work with a class-mate, talk with others in your community to gather information, or use the library or Internet to gather facts.

23-1. If there is a major conflict between the needs of a company and the needs of employees, should employees in the human resources department take the side of the business?

Reasons for "Yes"	Reasons for "No"

23-2. Are laws such as the Occupational Safety and Health Act and the Americans with Disabilities Act examples of too much government interference in business operations?

Reasons for "Yes"	Reasons for "No"

PROBLEMS

23-A. In the Answers column, write the letter of the human resources service in Column I that most closely matches the appropriate description of that service in Column II.

I. Human Resource Service	II. Description of Human Resources Activity	Answers
A. employment	1. Provides confidential personal problem solving, counseling, and support for employees.	_____
B. wages and benefits	2. Ensures effective communication and cooperation between management and employees.	_____
C. performance improvement	3. Plans and manages the financial and nonfinancial rewards available to employees.	_____
D. employee relations	4. Researches and maintains the information that managers need to determine personnel needs and manage the workforce.	_____
E. health and safety	5. Maintains an adequate number of qualified employees in the company.	_____
F. performance management	6. Trains and educates employees to ensure high quality and efficient work.	_____
G. employee assistance programs	7. Develops the evaluation system and materials and educates managers and employees on the proper methods for evaluating and improving performance. ...	_____
H. employment planning and research	8. Maintains safe work areas and work procedures, enforces laws and regulations related to safety and health, and provides adequate education and training in health and safety.	_____

23-B. Use the local newspaper or other sources of employment opportunities for your community. Identify a part-time or full-time job that is currently available, for which you are qualified, and that interests you. Clip or copy the advertisement to use as a reference. Complete the job application form that follows to apply for the job. Review the form carefully, plan your answers, and fill it out accurately and clearly. When you are finished, exchange your application with another student and discuss the strengths of the application and recommendations for improving it.

Job Application

Instructions: Print clearly in black or blue ink. Answer all questions. Sign and date the form.

PERSONAL INFORMATION:

Last Name _____ First Name _____ Middle Name _____

Street Address _____

City, State, Zip Code   Phone Number

_____   (_____)_____

Are you eligible to work in the United States? Yes _____ No _____

If you are under age 18, do you have an employment/age certificate? Yes _____ No _____

Have you been convicted of or pleaded no contest to a felony within the last five years? Yes _____ No _____

If yes, please explain: _____

_____

POSITION/AVAILABILITY:

Position Applied For   Part-Time   Full-Time

_____   _____   _____

Days/Hours Available

Monday _____ Tuesday _____ Wednesday _____ Thursday _____ Friday _____

Saturday _____ Sunday _____

Hours Available: From _____ To _____

What date are you available to start work?

_____

EDUCATION:

Name and Address of School - Degree/Diploma - Graduation Date

_____

_____

_____

Skills and Qualifications: List Specialized Skills and Any Related Training

_____

_____

Hobbies, Interests, Leadership, Awards, and Recognitions:

_____

_____

Continued

EMPLOYMENT HISTORY:

PRESENT OR LAST POSITION:

Employer: _____

Address: _____

Supervisor: _____ Phone: (_____)_____

Position Title: _____ From: _____ To: _____

Responsibilities: _____

Reason for Leaving: _____

May We Contact Your Present Employer? Yes _____ No _____

PREVIOUS POSITION:

Employer: _____

Address: _____

Supervisor: _____ Phone: (_____)_____

Position Title: _____ From: _____ To: _____

Responsibilities: _____

Reason for Leaving: _____

REFERENCES:

Name/Title - Address - Phone

_____

_____

_____

_____   _____
     Signature   Date

23-C. The following items describe steps to be taken in hiring employees. Number the steps to show the correct order for completing the employment procedures.

____ A.   Review applications to eliminate those applicants who do not meet minimum qualifications.

____ B.   Have applicants fill out an application form.

____ C.   Administer skills and knowledge tests.

____ D.   Hire the most qualified applicant.

____ E.   Establish a need to hire an employee (initiated by a manager).

____ F.   Conduct a general interview with applicants (by HR personnel).

____ G.   Provide orientation and initial training.

____ H.   Check the applicants' references, education, and past work experience.

____ I.   Prepare a job description and job specification.

____ J.   Interview applicants (by department manager and/or work team).

____ K.   Recruit applicants for the opening.

23-D. The human resources manager asked you to prepare a report on the employee turnover in your company over the last eight years. Use the data below to figure out the percentage of employee turnover based on the number of employees who left during the year.

Year	Average Number of Employees During the Year	Number of Employees Who Terminated Their Employment During the Year	Percentage of Employee Turnover
1	3,125	100	_____ %
2	3,455	112	_____ %
3	3,620	138	_____ %
4	3,580	122	_____ %
5	3,310	102	_____ %
6	3,150	144	_____ %
7	3,090	180	_____ %
8	3,200	105	_____ %

23-E. Obtain the classified section of a newspaper and clip an example of an employment advertisement that contains appropriate information for potential applicants. Next, clip an example of an ad that does not contain appropriate information. Attach both ads to this page in the space provided below. Below the ads, write why you believe the ads are good or poor.

Good Employment Ad	Poor Employment Ad

Reasons this ad is good:

_____

_____

_____

_____

_____

_____

Reasons this ad is poor:

_____

_____

_____

_____

_____

_____

23-F. If you are currently employed, use your job duties to complete the following job specification form. If you are not employed, interview a family member or friend who has a job and use that information to complete the form.

Job Specification Form

Company: _____ Department: _____

Job Title: _____ Rate of Pay: From _____ to _____

Previous Job in Organization: _____
Next Job in Organization: _____
Supervisor's Job Title: _____

QUALIFICATIONS
Education:

Experience:

Physical Requirements:

Specific Skills or Abilities Required:

Training Provided:

JOB REQUIREMENTS
Major Job Tasks:

Specific Job Duties:

Number of Work Hours Required per Week:
        Maximum _____ Minimum _____

Normal Work Schedule:
        Daily:

        Weekly:

Employee Benefits Provided:
        Vacation:

        Insurance:

        Other:

SMALL GROUP ACTIVITIES

With instructions from your teacher, divide into small groups and participate in the following activities.

New students in your school are similar to new employees in an organization. To help new employees adjust to the new work environment, many businesses offer new employee orientation sessions to acquaint a new hire with the policies and procedures of the business.

Group Activity 1

You have been asked by your principal to develop an orientation session for new students. Within your group, outline the information that should be included in this orientation session.

Group Activity 2

Your principal has asked you to develop questions for a follow-up interview with new students that will be conducted four to six weeks after the student enrolls. Develop a list of potential questions or discussion topics that would be appropriate to ask the new students. The goal is to see where improvements can be made to the orientation process.

Group Activity 3

Occasionally, students transfer from your school to another school during the school year. Develop a list of potential questions or discussion topics that would be appropriate to ask transferring students during an exit interview. Be prepared to share and discuss your answers with the class.

Study Guide

Part A—*Directions:* Indicate your answer to each of the following questions by writing either yes or no in the Answers column.

Answers

1. Does total employee compensation include both wages and benefits? .... 1. _____
2. On average, do companies spend an additional 15 percent of employee wages and salaries on benefits? .... 2. _____
3. Is a pension plan a company-sponsored retirement plan that makes regular payments to employees after retirement? .... 3. _____
4. Do federal and state laws require companies to offer a number of benefits to employees? 4. _____
5. Does "job sharing" mean that one person is prepared to complete the tasks required in two different jobs? .... 5. _____
6. If a business offers benefits to its employees, must it provide the identical set of benefits to all employees? .... 6. _____
7. Are some companies reducing their costs by contracting with outside companies to perform some human resources tasks? .... 7. _____
8. Does much of the cost of managing human resources go into the paperwork needed to gather and update employee information? .... 8. _____
9. Is one of the requirements for maintaining a high-quality workforce an effective system for performance review? .... 9. _____
10. Is a performance review the process of assessing how well the company is performing financially? .... 10. _____
11. Is the first step in developing a performance review process to design an evaluation form? 11. _____
12. Do managers usually conduct formal performance reviews of all employees once or twice a year? .... 12. _____
13. Should the scheduling of a performance review process be delayed for some time after performance has been evaluated to make the discussion more positive and objective? .... 13. _____
14. Should the manager and employee agree on a specific development plan for the next work period as a part of a performance review conference? .... 14. _____
15. In addition to the formal performance review procedures, should managers regularly provide informal feedback to every employee? .... 15. _____
16. Can formal training be conducted by supervisors, experienced employees, or professional trainers? .... 16. _____
17. Do U.S. companies spend $10–$20 million each year on formal training programs? .... 17. _____
18. Can companies justify the large allocation of money for training and development if employees are able to perform more and higher-quality work? .... 18. _____
19. On average, do companies spend several hundred dollars on every employee each year for training? .... 19. _____
20. Are all of the training needs of organizations obvious and easy to identify? .... 20. _____

Total Score _____

Part B—*Directions:* For each of the following statements, select the word, or group of words, that best completes the statement. In the Answers column, write the letter corresponding to the answer selected.

1. Pay based on an hourly rate is known as (a) salary, (b) wages, (c) piece rate, (d) commission.

1. _____

2. A system of policies and procedures for calculating the wages and salaries in an organization is a (a) performance review system, (b) human resources plan, (c) compensation plan, (d) payroll system. ....

2. _____

3. An individual employee's pay is based directly on the amount of work the employee produces in (a) a piece-rate plan, (b) a bonus plan (c) a wage and salary plan, (d) all of these plans. ....

3. _____

4. Paying an employee a bonus in addition to a small wage or salary is a variation of the (a) commission plan, (b) benefit plan, (c) wage plan, (d) combination plan. ....

4. _____

5. It is illegal for employers to pay less than an identified wage rate to any employee, according to (a) Social Security laws, (b) wage discrimination laws, (c) minimum wage laws, (d) equal employment opportunity laws. ....

5. _____

6. If employee contributions to a retirement plans are tax-deferred, (a) contributions are made before taxes are calculated on the employee's income, (b) taxes are paid by the employer rather than the employee, (c) the amount of the contribution must be reduced by the amount of the taxes owed, (d) all are these are correct. ....

6. _____

7. A program in which employees can select the benefits that meet their personal needs is known as (a) a choice plan, (b) a cafeteria plan, (c) a flexible plan, (d) an option plan. ......

7. _____

8. Contracting with an information systems company to manage all the personnel data required to manage human resources is an example of (a) downsizing (b) joint management, (c) outsourcing, (d) job sharing. ....

8. _____

9. Which of the following is NOT a guideline for a manager to follow in preparing for an effective performance review conference? (a) Focus the discussion on the employee and not on the employee's performance. (b) Allow the employee opportunities to discuss his or her performance and views of the job, working conditions, and available support. (c) Discuss strengths as well as areas that need improvement. (d) Provide copies of the information that will be reviewed in advance. ....

9. _____

10. The common types of training provided by U.S. employers include all of the following EXCEPT (a) employee health and wellness training, (b) basic skills training, (c) job skills training, (d) all of these are common types of training provided. ....

10. _____

Total Score _____

Part C—*Directions:* In the Answers column, write the letter of the term in Column I that most closely matches each statement in Column II.

Column I	Column II	Answers
A. bonus	1. Pays the employee a fixed rate for each unit produced	_____
B. commission	2. Money paid at the end of a specific but long period of time for performance that exceeds the expected standard for that period	_____
C. piece-rate	3. Pay based on a time frame other than hourly, such as weekly or monthly	_____
D. profit sharing	4. Pays employees a percentage of the volume of sales for which they are responsible	_____
E. salary	5. Pays employees a small percentage of the company's profits at the end of the year	_____

Total Score _____

Directions: Study each controversial issue carefully. Follow the advice of your teacher before listing in the columns provided reasons why people might answer Yes or No. Your teacher may want you to work with a classmate, talk with others in your community to gather information, or use the library or Internet to gather facts.

24-1. Because employee compensation is one of the highest costs to most businesses, should employers try to pay employees the lowest amount possible in compensation and benefits that does not result in a high turnover rate?

Reasons for "Yes"	Reasons for "No"

24-2. Should individual employees rather than employers be responsible for determining, obtaining, and paying for the education and training they will need to improve their employability and productivity?

Reasons for "Yes"	Reasons for "No"

PROBLEMS

24-A. The Storeze Company employs six salespeople to sell its products. Last year, each salesperson sold the following amounts:

Salesperson	Amount of Sales	Straight Salary	Commission	Salary and Bonus
Jackson	$569,000			
Klein	$630,000			
Drase	$520,500			
Teng	$605,200			
Russo	$723,000			
Astor	$502,600			
Total salary costs				

The company is considering several pay plans. Salespeople are currently paid a straight salary of $27,000 a year. Proposed pay plans are (1) a straight commission of 4.5 percent on all sales, and (2) a salary of $20,000 plus a bonus of 9 percent on all sales above $500,000.

1. Complete the table to show the salary of each salesperson for the three pay plans. Also compute the cost of each plan for the company.
2. Write a recommendation for the company in which you justify one of the plans based on the chart's information.

_____

_____

_____

_____

24-B. Complete the following chart illustrating the costs of fringe benefits for six companies.

Company	Total Payroll	Fringe Benefit % of Total Payroll	Fringe Benefit Costs	Total Payroll and Benefits
A	$ 960,000	32.00%	$	$
B		28.50%		$1,350,000
C	$ 495,000		$170,775	
D		30.00%	$ 36,500	
E	$ 827,600			$ 910,000
F		25.00%		$1,500,000

24-C. Based on the minimum wage rate in effect in 2006 for each of the states listed in the following table, calculate the amount earned by an employee earning the minimum wage for the total hours worked during one week. If a state's minimum wage rate is lower than the federal minimum rate, assume the job is one that is exempt from federal regulation. Also assume that the employee earns 1½ times the regular wage rate for hours worked above 40.

State	2006 Minimum Wage	Hours Worked	Amount Earned
California	$6.75	38	
Colorado	$6.85	29	
Connecticut	$7.40	48	
Georgia	$5.15	40	
Kansas	$2.65	44	
Nevada	$6.15	33	
Oregon	$7.50	40	
Washington	$7.63	23	
Wisconsin	$5.70	39	

24-D. You have been asked to help a human resources manager evaluate several alternatives for restructuring the total compensation plan for a large company. The manager is concerned about the rapidly increasing costs of wages and benefits, yet also realizes that the amount and type of compensation are important factors that employees consider when selecting a job. Consider the following three alternatives, and describe the advantage of each alternative (a) to the employer and (b) to employees. Then recommend the alternative you believe would be best for the company in terms of controlling the rising costs of wages and benefits.

Alternative A: Maintain the same level of increases in wages and salaries but cut expensive employee benefits.

Advantages to the Employer: _____

_____

_____

Advantages to Employees: _____

_____

_____

Alternative B: Reduce the amount of wage and salary increases but pay a higher amount for increases in the costs of employee benefits.

Advantages to the Employer: _____

_____

_____

_____

Advantages to Employees: _____

_____

_____

_____

Alternative C: Reduce the amount of wage and salary increases and the amount of the employer contributions to the cost of employee benefits but offer employees a choice of benefits under a cafeteria plan as well as the choice to take the amount the employer normally pays for benefits as an end-of-year bonus rather than as a benefit.

Advantages to the Employer: _____

_____

_____

_____

Advantages to Employees: _____

_____

_____

_____

Recommended Alternative: _____

Rationale: _____

_____

_____

24-E. Contributions to an employee retirement plan can be tax-deferred, meaning that the contributions are made to the retirement plan before an employee's taxes are calculated. However, taxes will have to be paid as the contributions are withdrawn during the employee's retirement. Because the income of most retired persons is lower than when they were employed, the taxes will be paid at a lower rate. Complete the following table to determine the amount of tax that each employee would have paid if the annual retirement contributions were not tax-deferred, and the amount of tax savings realized if contributions were tax-deferred and paid at the reduced tax rate at retirement.

Employee	Annual Retirement Contribution	Current Tax Rate	Tax Rate at Retirement	Taxes Paid if Contributions are Not Tax-Deferred	Tax Savings if Contributions are Tax-Deferred
A	$ 1,845	15%	10%		
B	$10,860	28%	25%		
C	$13,209	33%	28%		
D	$ 2,520	10%	0%		
E	$40,440	35%	28%		

24-F. A review was completed of the outsourcing agreements made by 124 large companies to determine what human resources activities were most frequently outsourced. The following results were reported:

Human Resources Activity	Number of Companies Outsourcing	Percentage
Payroll	108	_____
Administering information systems	103	_____
Benefits management	101	_____
Regulatory compliance	83	_____
Compensation planning	60	_____
Recruiting and interviewing	52	_____
Performance management	45	_____
Training and development	40	_____

1. Complete the table by filling in the percentage of companies surveyed who outsource each activity.
2. In the space below, construct a bar chart that illustrates the use of outsourcing in human resources management.

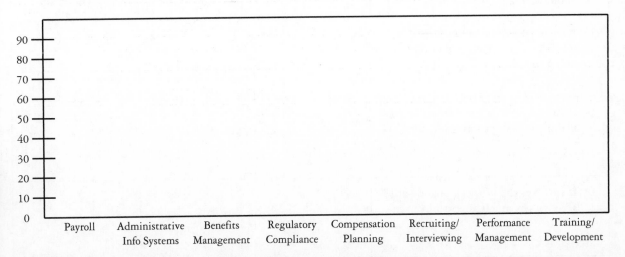

24-G. Column I lists the characteristics of effective training based on Figure 24-3 in the chapter. In Column II, write a benefit the trainee receives from training as a result of each characteristic that will improve the results of the training.

Column I: Characteristic of Effective Training	Column II: Results in improved employee performance because...
1. It is interesting to the trainee.	
2. It is related to knowledge the trainee already has developed.	
3. It explains why as well as how something is done.	
4. It progresses from simple to more difficult steps.	
5. It allows the trainee to learn complicated procedures in small steps.	
6. It allows the trainee plenty of practice time.	
7. It allows the trainee to concentrate on becoming comfortable with a new procedure before worrying about accuracy.	
8. It provides regular and positive feedback to the trainee on progress being made.	
9. It can be done in short time blocks using a variety of activities.	
10. It involves the learner in hands-on activities as much as possible.	

SMALL GROUP ACTIVITIES

Group Activity 1

With instructions from your teacher, divide into small groups of four to six students. Identify three people from each of the following age groups who currently hold part-time or full-time jobs. Identify the type of job that each person holds. Ask each person the following questions about the compensation and benefits he or she receives and record the responses. Be prepared to define the compensation and benefits terms used in the questions.

1. Is the compensation you receive a salary or a wage?

_____

_____

2. Is any or all of your compensation based on your performance, such as a commission or piece rate? If so, how is the compensation calculated?

_____

_____

3. Do you believe your level of compensation adequately reflects the quantity and quality of work you perform for your employer? Why or why not?

_____

_____

4. If you could improve the compensation system in your company, what recommendations would you make?

_____

_____

5. Do you receive any paid benefits from your employer? If so, what benefits do you receive? If not, do other employees at your job receive benefits? How does an employee qualify to receive benefits?

_____

_____

6. How important are employee benefits to you at this point in your life? Which types of benefits are most important to you, and which are least important to you?

_____

_____

7. If you could improve the benefits system in your company, what recommendations would you make?

_____

_____

As a group, review the answers you received. Note differences in responses based on the age of the respondents and the type of job held. Are there any other characteristics of respondents that seem to make a difference in the responses they provided?

Summarize the information you collected and prepare a brief oral report for presentation to the class. Use a computer to prepare visual aids to support your presentation.

Group Activity 2

With instructions from your teacher, divide into groups of three. You will role-play a performance review conference with one team member playing the role of the supervisor, another the role of the employee, and the third team member observing the role-play, taking notes, providing feedback, and leading a team discussion after the role-play is complete.

Before beginning the role-play, the team should prepare by choosing roles and then creating a scenario for the role-play. The scenario should be a description of the job being evaluated and a list of the main strengths and areas for improvement that will be included in the discussion. Then the manager and employee should spend some time alone planning for the conference. The observer should review information in the chapter about an effective performance review conference and look for those things during the role-play. The role-play should last four or five minutes, and each person should try to be as realistic as possible in the role they are playing.

When the role-play is complete, the observer should provide feedback on the strengths of the conference and the ways it might be improved. Team members in the role-play should discuss the feelings they had during the conference and how they felt after it was complete. If time permits, team members should change roles and complete additional role-plays.

<table>
<tr><td rowspan="3">Chapter 25

Developing an
Effective
Organization</td><td rowspan="2">Name _____</td><td colspan="5" align="center">Scoring Record</td></tr>
<tr><td></td><td>Part A</td><td>Part B</td><td>Part C</td><td>Total</td></tr>
<tr><td rowspan="2">Date _____</td><td>Perfect score</td><td>20</td><td>10</td><td>5</td><td>35</td></tr>
<tr><td></td><td>My score</td><td></td><td></td><td></td><td></td></tr>
</table>

Study Guide

Part A—*Directions:* Indicate your answer to each of the following questions by writing either yes or no in the Answers column.

Answers

1. Were a number of companies forced to restructure and downsize in the last part of the twentieth century? .... 1. _____

2. Is job security the likelihood that a worker will continue to be employed by the same company in the future? .... 2. _____

3. Do free-trade agreements reduce barriers on the sale of goods and services between countries? .... 3. _____

4. Is organizational development a term used to describe programs that match the long-term career planning of employees with the employment needs of the business? .... 4. _____

5. Is an important objective of organizational development to improve work processes? ...... 5. _____

6. Is the reason a previously successful business fails likely to be the inability to change? .... 6. _____

7. Is affirming the organization's mission and goals the first step in planning and implementing an organizational development program? .... 7. _____

8. Are customer service standards specific statements of the expected results from critical business activities? .... 8. _____

9. Is it easier to create change in an organization when only the employees who are affected by the change are informed of the change? .... 9. _____

10. Can organizational changes be successful even if they are not accepted as the new culture of the organization? .... 10. _____

11. Are most employees concerned only with the amount of their paycheck and benefits? ..... 11. _____

12. Does job design refer to the kinds of tasks that make up a job and the way workers perform these tasks in doing their jobs? .... 12. _____

13. Should companies enlarge jobs to reduce the number of employees needed? .... 13. _____

14. Do the company and the employees benefit if the company trains employees for more than one job in the company, even though they typically perform only one? .... 14. _____

15. Do managers who practice job enrichment allow their employees to make decisions about their work? .... 15. _____

16. In the past, did many companies terminate employees who were not needed, without considering future employment needs? .... 16. _____

17. Must career paths move an employee from an entry-level position into management? ..... 17. _____

18. Is it necessary for the human resources department to make long-term projections about the company's employment needs in order to support career planning? .... 18. _____

19. Should each job in a company be part of a career path? .... 19. _____

20. Should all career development programs in a company be available to all employees? ...... 20. _____

Total Score   _____

Part B—*Directions:* For each of the following statements, select the word, or group of words, that best completes the statement. In the Answers column, write the letter corresponding to the answer selected.

Answers

1. When human resources departments help employees match their career plans with the employment needs of the business, they are involved in (a) organizational development, (b) restructuring, (c) career development, (d) employee evaluation. .... 1. _____

2. When employees are encouraged to participate in important decision making in the business, they are involved in (a) cross training, (b) job design, (c) job enrichment, (d) labor relations. .... 2. _____

3. In the past, the attitude of many companies toward employees was (a) you have a job for life, (b) if you are not needed, you will be terminated, (c) we will hire only part-time employees, (d) we will give you regular promotions. .... 3. _____

4. Which of the following is needed for an effective career development program? (a) career paths, (b) effective employee evaluation, (c) employee training, (d) all of these are needed. 4. _____

5. Traditional career paths moved employees (a) into other companies, (b) into dead-end jobs, (c) toward management positions, (d) into highly technical positions. .... 5. _____

6. The document that identifies the jobs that are part of the employee's career path, the training needed to advance along the career path, and a tentative schedule for the plan's activities is the (a) performance review, (b) evaluation plan, (c) job specification, (d) career plan. 6. _____

7. The responsibility for managing a career development program rests with (a) the human resources department, (b) department managers, (c) each employee, (d) the company's chief executive officer. .... 7. _____

8. Which of the following is NOT true of business careers? (a) People who begin a business career in one industry can easily transfer to another industry. (b) Business careers require a high level of skill, education, and experience. (c) Business career paths do not require you to move into management. (d) Business careers are appealing because of the number and variety of jobs available. .... 8. _____

9. The level of employment that requires extensive understanding of the operations of a specific company or industry is (a) an entry-level occupation, (b) a specialist occupation, (c) a team leader, (d) an executive/entrepreneur. .... 9. _____

10. A career portfolio should include (a) examples of school projects you have completed, (b) checklists of competencies you have mastered, (c) performance reviews from employers, (d) all of these items. .... 10. _____

Total Score _____

Part C—*Directions:* In the Answers column, write the letter of the term in Column I that most closely matches each statement in Column II.

Column I	Column II	Answers
A. career path	1. An organized collection of information and materials developed to represent yourself, your preparation, and your accomplishments	_____
B. career plan		
C. job design	2. A progression of related jobs with increasing skill requirements and responsibility	_____
D. job enrichment	3. Giving employees the authority to make meaningful decisions about their work	_____
E. portfolio	4. Identifies the jobs that are part of the employee's career path, the training and development needed to advance along the career path, and a tentative schedule	_____
	5. The kinds of tasks that make up a job and the way workers perform these tasks in doing their jobs	_____

Total Score _____

Directions: Study each controversial issue carefully. Follow the advice of your teacher before listing in the columns provided reasons why people might answer Yes or No. Your teacher may want you to work with a classmate, talk with others in your community to gather information, or use the library or Internet to gather facts.

25-1. Employee work teams are often given the responsibility to schedule work, assign responsibilities to team members, schedule vacations, and even hire and fire members of the work team. Should employees in nonmanagerial positions be given these responsibilities and authority over their peers?

Reasons for "Yes"	Reasons for "No"

25-2. When employees are hired in many Japanese firms, they usually remain with the company for as long as they choose, provided they perform effectively. U.S. firms often have a high rate of employee turnover with much less loyalty to employees. Should U.S. companies adopt a philosophy like those of Japanese firms?

Reasons for "Yes"	Reasons for "No"

PROBLEMS

25-A. Using the Internet, business magazines, or newspapers, locate an article about a business facing a problem requiring major change. Use the list of indicators in Figure 25-1 in the textbook to guide your research. Read the article, and write a one-paragraph description of the problem.

Assume you are a manager in charge of organizational development for an organization facing the problem you described. Follow the steps for planning and implementing an organizational development program listed in the chapter to describe how you would solve the problem. Prepare a two-page report describing the solution and the procedure you would follow.

25-B. A recent survey was completed of 823 employees involved in work teams that are responsible for the day-to-day decisions for their work areas. When asked to identify the main barriers to developing effective work teams, they listed the following factors:

Barrier	% of Respondents	No. of Respondents
Insufficient training	54%	_____
Supervisor resistance	47%	_____
Incompatible policies	47%	_____
Lack of planning	40%	_____
Lack of management support	31%	_____
Lack of recognition	24%	_____

1. Complete the table above by calculating the number of employees who identified each of the barriers. Then prepare a bar chart that illustrates the findings from the survey.

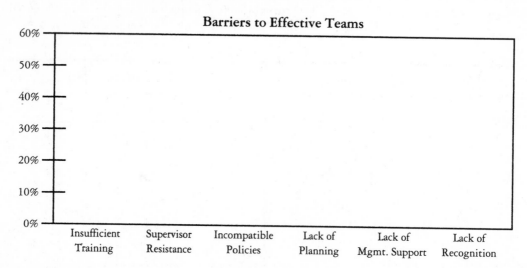

2. Prepare three recommendations for managers on what the company should do to increase the chances that work teams will be effective.

_____

_____

_____

25-C. Conduct a survey of five people who have worked full-time for less than two years and five people who have worked full-time for more than ten years. Ask each person the following questions:

	Very Important	Somewhat Important	Uncertain	Somewhat Unimportant	Very Unimportant
1. How important is job security to you?	_____	_____	_____	_____	_____
2. How important is employee involvement in critical work decisions to you?	_____	_____	_____	_____	_____

After you have completed the surveys, prepare a bar graph to illustrate your results, comparing the responses of the two groups. Then combine your results with the results of your classmates. Discuss the findings and the implications for organizational development in businesses.

Bar Graph

25-D. Traditional career paths in business have evolved from entry-level positions requiring limited amounts of education and experience to management positions requiring advanced education and experience. Today, new career paths are available allowing those employees who do not choose a career in management to advance into more specialized careers with greater responsibilities.

Using the classified advertising of a newspaper or an Internet site that provides job listings, identify three different jobs that you believe would form a career ladder that would move a person from entry level to a management position. Complete the chart on the left with the required information for each job. Then prepare another career ladder to identify a sequence of jobs leading to greater responsibilities in nonmanagement positions. Complete the chart on the right with the required information.

When you have completed the two career ladders, list the advantages and disadvantages of a management versus a nonmanagement career path based on the information you collected.

Management Career Ladder	Nonmanagement Career Ladder
Beginning Job Job title: Major duties: Education: Experience:	**Beginning Job** Job title: Major duties: Education: Experience:
2nd-Level Job Job title: Major duties: Education: Experience:	**2nd-Level Job** Job title: Major duties: Education: Experience:
3rd-Level Job Job title: Major duties: Education: Experience:	**3rd-Level Job** Job title: Major duties: Education: Experience:

Advantages of a management career path: _____

_____

_____

Disadvantages of a management career path: _____

_____

_____

25-E. International business is expanding and offering exciting and rewarding opportunities for people who carefully plan and prepare for international careers. Preparation involves obtaining the appropriate education, training, and experience, which may take several years and a progression through a number of jobs.

Using the library or the Internet, research a career area that can lead to a job in international business. Choose one area you would like to investigate, and develop a career path for yourself beginning now. If possible, identify jobs in the career path that fit each of the five employment levels described in Chapter 25 of the text. List additional education you will need, special training required, and the amount and type of work experience needed to qualify for each job. Prepare this information in both written form and on a timeline for presentation to your class.

Career Area in International Business _____

Entry-Level Job _____
Education Required   **Special Training Required**   **Experience Required**

Career-Level Job _____
Education Required   **Special Training Required**   **Experience Required**

Specialist Job _____
Education Required   **Special Training Required**   **Experience Required**

Supervisor/Management Job _____
Education Required   **Special Training Required**   **Experience Required**

Executive/Entrepreneur Job _____
Education Required   **Special Training Required**   **Experience Required**

Timeline

SMALL GROUP ACTIVITIES

With instructions from your teacher, divide into small groups and participate in the following activities. Your team will function as the members of a work group in a business that has empowered teams with day-to-day management responsibilities. You know your group can be no more effective than the work and efforts of each team member. Your goal is to solve problems presented to you so that the team works together effectively and is the most effective work group it can be.

Group Activity 1

Many organizations today are relying on work teams to take responsibility for the day-to-day operations and decisions of their work areas. Team members meet together to plan, make decisions, solve problems, and ensure their work group achieves its goals. Organizations have found that members of effective teams develop a strong loyalty to the other members and take personal responsibility for the effective operation of the team and the quality of its work. As a team, you are presented with the following situations involving the performance of a team member. Discuss each situation and develop a plan for resolving the problem in the most effective way possible.

1. A team member who is responsible for preparing customer invoices has a history of making errors in totaling the amounts on the invoices. Each invoice is double-checked by at least one other team member, so that the errors are found and corrected before the invoices are mailed. Since the employee has a large number of invoices to complete each day, it appears she hurries, knowing someone else will correct the mistakes.

2. A very experienced employee is responsible for operating a machine that punches holes through metal plates one-inch thick. A safety shield is supposed to be lowered in place each time the punch is operated. The employee has found that more plates can be punched if the shield is not used. The team has a record of no injuries on the job and has received recognition by the company for that record. The team knows that if the employee's hands are caught in the press, a serious injury will result, but the employee believes his experience allows him to work without the safety shield in place.

3. A new employee who has been a member of the work group for four weeks is having trouble organizing her work. She is very effective at performing her work once she is organized, but spends a great deal of time finding materials and supplies and determining how she will approach each task. She seems reluctant to ask for help and seems to want to work on her own more than with the team.

4. A young employee who is a recent immigrant to the United States seems to be very shy around coworkers. He seldom speaks to them, does not sit with them at lunch, and seldom goes on breaks with anyone he works with. It does not seem to affect the quality of the work he does by himself, but his work is not as effective when he has a task that requires him to work with others. He has a nice personality and wants to get along, but seems to be afraid that others might not want to associate with him.

Group Activity 2

Work teams are responsible for their effectiveness—both as a team and of each team member. Often, training needs can be identified from the areas where employees are not performing as well as expected, and the work group may want to undertake formal or informal training. The training may be provided to one or a few team members, or it might be appropriate for the entire team. It could involve a short, informal experience or participation in a formal training activity. The training could be provided by team members, or the team may request that training be offered by a manager, a training specialist, or a person from the organization who has expertise in the area requiring training.

Review each of the four situations in Group Activity 1. Your team should review each scenario and identify one or more possible training needs that appear to exist. Then describe how training could be offered that you believe would be effective in improving employee performance.

Possible Training Need	Recommended Training Procedures
1.	1.
2.	2.
3.	3.
4.	4.